# *Gone Fishin'...*

## For Hybrid Bass

For Roe Foster          8/6/09

These Cowalskie's know
how to swim!

Enjoy —

*John Korn, Jr. of Flemington, New Jersey with a beauty of a Spruce Run Reservoir Rocket.*

# *Gone Fishin'...*

# For Hybrid Bass

## By Manny Luftglass

**Foreword By Bill Baab**
**Midword By Bruce Condello**
**Afterword By Ronald L. Bern**

Gone Fishin' Enterprises
PO Box 556, Annandale, New Jersey 08801

**Pictured on the cover:**

(Left) Guide Jay Clementi. Jay caught and released this 10½ pound hybrid
at J. Percy Priest Lake in Tennessee on an Orvis fly rod,
using a Jay Rabbit Strip Diver. Photo courtesy Jay Clementi.

(Middle) Author and grand-daughter Madison Zook about to release
an 8-pound hybrid caught at Spruce Run Reservoir in New Jersey.
Photo courtesy of dad, Greg Zook.

(Right) Dave Kittaka, an Indiana Fisheries Biologist, holding an
11-pound hybrid caught while trolling a stick-bait,
before releasing back into Lake Monroe. Photo courtesy of Brian Schoenung.

**Pictured on the back cover:**

Max Howard, age 6, got tired of fishing at the "Airport Lake" near Palm Beach
Airport, Florida, so his dad Willie, Outdoors Editor of the *Palm Beach Post*
let Max pull a lure behind his remote-controlled boat, and sure enough,
this modest sunshine bass sunk the boat and they had to go out and
rescue boat and fish. Photo courtesy Willie Howard.

**Gone Fishin' ... For Hybrid Bass**

By Manny Luftglass

© 2005 Emanuel Luftglass

*Published By*
**Gone Fishin' Enterprises**
PO Box 556, Annandale, New Jersey 08801

ISBN: 0-9755797-3-8

UPC: 793380 86321 0

**Photo Credits:**

Phil Chapman, Brady Jenkins, Joe Bauer Sr., Doug Darr, guide Jimmy Johnson, Robin Knox,
Ted Boilleau, Robert Miller, Chris Larson, Bruce Condello, Col. Jesse Duncan, Dave Hickman,
Tom Holman, Randy Noyes, Craig Condello, Dan Hannum, John Korn Sr., Doug Stang, Mike's B&T,
John Navarro, guide Clarence Boatman, guide Jeff Knapp, guide Buster Green,
Tim Churchill, guide Butch Terpe, Jeremy Adams, Tom Hampton, Scott Morrison.

**Design & Typography:**
TeleSet, Hillsborough, New Jersey

PRINTED IN THE UNITED STATES

*DEDICATION*

*This one is pretty easy. I have busted on folks in government
for many a year.*

*But having been in government myself for a while,
I realize that this is a silly thing to do when, by and large,
most of the people who work for the various departments of
Fish and Game/Wildlife/Boating in America are true public
servants who do their job in silent anonymity. So to all those
wonderful nameless and faceless people who work for us
everywhere, I dedicate this book to you!*

*To the people who stumble down embankments stocking the
fish, those who clean out the growing ponds, the folks who
squeeze the roe and sperm out of breeders to create yet
another massive number of fry, this book is for you. You
deserve what my friend John Gusciora, a former cop with the
Somerville, N.J. Police Department used to describe as an
"Attaboy," so to you all: Attaboy, okay?*

*Kids with striper hybrids at Tenoroc Fish Management Area, Lakeland, Florida.*

Photos by Phil Chapman

# Contents

# Introduction to Foreword

*Bill Baab is a former OWAA member and lifetime Georgia Outdoor Writers Association member, plus a life member of BASS and the National Fresh water Fishing Hall of Fame. He retired as Outdoor Editor of* The Augusta, Georgia Chronicle, *and currently is its fishing editor. And during his spare time, he, his wife Bea and their dog, Princess Augusta Tickletummy, can be found fishing for hybrid bass on Clarks Hill Reservoir, Georgia.*

*Photo by Bea Baab*

# Foreword

## *By Bill Baab*

"In the beginning, a South Carolina Wildlife Resources Department fisheries biologist created the hybrid bass in 1965, but it took the cooperation of a Tennessee state fisheries scientist to bring the experiment crossbreed to its present level of piscatorial popularity.

It was Dr. Robert E. Stevens who was thrilled to observe some 70,000 fry after he crossed a white bass male and striped bass female at South Carolina's Moncks Corner striped bass hatchery.

But Stevens did not have the facilities to rear the fish past the fry state so Tennessee's Dave Bishop, who also had been working on the hybrid idea, entered the scene. Bishop stocked about half of those fry into Cherokee Lake[1] just after Easter of 1965 and by the

---

[1] *This is discussed later on in the Tennessee section.*

time fall had rolled around, anglers were catching 10-12 ounce hybrids. The following spring, the rapidly growing fish weighed 1½ pounds and by the fall of 1966, 18 month-old hybrids weighing 2½ pounds were being caught by excited fishermen.

Fishermen weren't just excited-they were going crazy about catching a fish that pulled like a runaway freight train. Not only did it pull good, it tasted good, too, and had all the attributes of its "mother" striped bass, but few of its "daddy" white bass. The white bass also was a strong puller, but hybrids were even stronger. Best of all, hybrids schooled in great numbers, just like their parent fish.

My home lake of Clarks Hill Reservoir, a 70,000-acre Corp. of Engineers impoundment on the Savannah River, was stocked with more than 3,600,000 hybrid fry in the spring of 1967. Soon, what happened in the Tennessee lake was being replicated at Clarks Hill.

It was during the spring of 1968, while searching for acres — huge schools of white bass moving up lake tributaries on spawning runs, that I caught my first hybrid. It struck a white inline spinner called a Shyster and I knew whatever it was, it wasn't a white bass. Careful not to make the mistake many fishermen made, I kept my spinning reel's drag loose, but tight enough to have some control over the fish, which was making long and powerful runs. I could even feel it shaking its head like a bulldog, but finally persuaded the 2-pounder to be netted. It pulled like it weighed 10 pounds.

"What the heck is this?" I wondered at the time because I wasn't thinking about the hybrids I'd first written about in 1966, two years after becoming outdoor editor of *The Augusta Georgia Chronicle*. Broken lines above and below the fish's lateral line told me it wasn't a striped bass, whose main line patterns are mostly solid. Then I remembered and my fishing life changed from that day.

Introduction of hybrids into other states' lakes changed a lot of angler's lives and you can join the fun, too, by reading *Gone Fishin'... For Hybrids*. Author Manny Luftglass takes you on a state-by-state hybrid bass tour and tells you all you need to know to join the legions of hybrid hunters."

## CHAPTER 1

# A Whole Book About One Fish? Why?

S imply, because they break lines! And because they snaps rods. And because they rip poles out of unsuspecting anglers hands. And because they tear rods out of boats!

As I began to formulate my thinking on how I could explain why I wanted to write a book about this one particular fish, I figured that I had better come up with a good excuse. Certainly I needed one that went deeper than my original idea. You see, my original idea was based on the simple fact that I personally would rather catch a hybrid bass than any one other single fish in the whole wide world!

And I've caught lots of other fine critters, for sure. They include a wide variety of other bass, but for me, as much as I enjoy catching "other" bass, there really is only one kind that I want. Include in that list calico bass ("crappie"), rock bass, largemouth and smallmouth bass, striped bass, yellow bass, white bass, and a whole gang of saltwater fish that are also referred to as "bass" from time to time.

But for those of you who have already caught one single, for-real "hybrid" bass, you probably already know why I wanted to write a book about them, because they are, pound-for-pound, the fightingest critter in all of these United States!

Many an angler has his own preferred bass. Some like

crappie/calico, because they are usually easy to catch, can be found in large schools, and taste real fine. Ditto the less commonly found rock bass.

Down south, white and yellow bass are smaller fish which fight well but again, the focus here is on the word "smaller." The more serious guys want largemouth bass because they grow to large size, hit lures with abandon, and jump like the dickens. Smallmouth lovers want their fish for the same reasons as "bucket mouth" bass enthusiasts do, and swear that their "bronze backs" fight much better than largemouth bass do.

And then we have the contingent of folks who want the biggest bass available, and clearly, true-strain striped bass fit that bill to a tee. Freshwater stripers grow to enormous size, upwards of 50 plus pounds in many states, and so far, no hybrid has come near that size. Frankly, if any ever do, chances are good to excellent that true-strain striper purists might get a hankering to try my Rockets from time to time.

I have toyed with bass lovers at a variety of fishing seminars that I have given on the subject of hybrid bass. Poking fun is always okay if no one gets near enough to hit me hard so I do this when I have enough distance between me and the fellow who is wearing a bunch of those all-to-familiar bass club patches. But in all honesty, I really do feel that a five pound hybrid bass can tow any other ten pound bass around without even knowing that something is dragging behind it.

Of course I have never caught a peacock bass, which I hear equals the strength and speed of hybrid bass but if and when I do, and this book sells out, I may have to add a post script about that tropical beauty called peacock. We have lots of them in South Florida.

~

CHAPTER 2

# What's The Difference?

F ar and away, the main difference between striped bass, hybrid striped bass, white bass and yellow bass is the size. True "striped" bass grow bigger by a lot then any of the other threesome. But you can catch small true-strains, especially in brackish water or in pure saltwater. I've also caught little stripers in a place like Lake Mead. But the other big difference is that hybrid bass fight much longer and harder than a true-strain of similar weight, and you can take that to the bank.

Yellow bass have a yellowish glow to them and are also far smaller than the other three. And a white bass may reach a couple of pounds or even more and sure can fight, but it only has one stripe that runs clear across its body in a horizontal line. True-strain stripers have lots of unbroken lines that run from head to tail and again, are bigger and slimmer than hybrids, unless you catch a "cow" which could weight 40 pounds or more. Again though, straight lines from end to end, got it? On the other hand, hybrid bass will have a series of broken lines that go from one end to the other and they will be far fatter than their true-strain relatives and, ooh, do they ever break rods and monofilament or what?

Photo by Phil Chapman, Florida F&WCC.

*Striped bass parent (top), white bass parent (bottom),
and hybrid bass offspring (middle).*

## CHAPTER 3

# What's In A Name?

Hybrid bass is the most commonly used name for these fish. They are called hybrid because as a cross-breed of two fish, white bass and striped bass, the end result is a fish that cannot breed, thus the word "hybrid." I've heard that there may be historical data that has proven that some hybrid bass have been known to reproduce, but I have never actually seen it proven. I release 90 plus % of the Rockets that I catch, but from time to time, I have cleaned a few that contain either roe or sperm but folks tell me that they still aren't able to mix their stuff together and create offspring.

Here's a few of the nicknames I have stumbled across as I did the research for this book, and for sure, there must be plenty more. Of course an angler who gets busted off can very quickly create a new name, something like ">[;!Doggone #!@_/?! Critter," but the main alternates include these:

**Rocket!** My name, I think, one that I gave to these fish back in the 90's when I started catching them in serious numbers. I call 'em "Rocket" because they hit like one. And because they fight like one. And because they swim with the speed of one. And because they can turn and change direction on a dime, just like a rocket can.

**Pocket Rocket.** Youngsters will associate the term Rocket with

Roger Clemens but old timers who were hockey fans may remember when a star player named Maurice Richard was called the Rocket. And then his younger brother (or maybe his son?) came along and got the moniker Pocket Rocket. So I call smaller hybrid bass Pocket Rockets, got it?

**Whiper.** Simple — a combination of the two fish, **WHI**te bass and striped (stri**PER**) bass. (I still like Rocket)

**Wiper.** Ditto the above, just with the "h" left out, maybe the most common nickname.

**Reciprocal Cross.** Most hybrid bass have been created by mixing the roe of a female true-strain striper with the sperm of a male white bass. But my friend, Walt Murawski who was with the New Jersey Department of Fish and Wildlife for many years once told me that when the reversal was done, crossing a male striper with a female white, the term "reciprocal" was given to this end result.

**Sunshine Bass.** While "wiper" may be the best known nickname, "Sunshine" comes in a pretty close second. I suppose my second home, Florida, may take credit for this nickname but it is used in quite a few other states. Some feel that a "Sunshine" bass is a mix of a female striper and a male white but then again, a few feel that it is the other way around. I suppose it depends on where you live.

**Palmetto Bass.** Again, another name that gets confused because some feel that a Palmetto is a mix of a female white and a male striper but still more think it's the reverse mix as with a "Sunshine." Folks in Kansas like this name mainly. And you know what? Who cares, they all fight great!

**Cherokee Bass.** A name used most often in Tennessee, but applied elsewhere as well.

**"Stripes"** One of the names applied to these fish in Alabama.

**Whiterock Bass.** It's heard in a few states. Easy to understand, mix a WHITE bass with what anglers call stripers in a variety of states, "ROCK", and you get whiterock, got it?

**SWH.** Often used by state fish and game guys as an abbreviation for Striped bass/White bass Hybrids, understand?

**Hybrid Striped Bass.** Can be heard in some locales.

**Striper.** The most commonly heard mistake name because a whole bunch of fishermen confuse hybrids with stripers and they are really two completely different critters. But, sorry striper enthusiasts, my Rocket is faster and stronger then "stripers" are.

**Bodie Bass.** I heard that this is used by some fishermen in Arkansas and maybe a few in North Carolina as well. And why "bodie?" Honestly, I don't know.

**Football with Fins.** Frankly, I don't remember if I heard that elsewhere or just had it appear in a dream. Chances are that someone else coined this excellent term though.

Rice Krispies could be another name I could use, if and when I find out that someone else invented the nickname Rocket before me. I used to think that I created the name "Whiper" as a conjunction of the words white bass and striper but then I found out that it had already been coined before I did it. And that's when I started to use Rocket. But if you want another name, try Rice Krispies because they surely do create all three of the sounds often attributed to that super cereal.

"Snap?" Imagine your rod breaking on a sudden lunge. "Crackle?" This sound can be heard in a silent sundown as your line crackles away, ripping across the top of the water on a lunatic run. And "Pop?" Hey simple, lines go pop all day long as unsuspecting anglers fish with too tight a drag.

I was told by a friend with the Florida Fish and Game department that the American Fisheries Society calls them both Sunshine and Palmetto bass. Hey AFS, try Rocket!

## CHAPTER 4

# In General

## Bait

Just imagine an "eating machine," and you have hybrid bass. That name is often attributed to barracuda and bluefish in the ocean. Well, in freshwater, hybrid bass will eat doggone near anything they can catch. This includes live and dead bait, with fish alone making up the majority of their diet.

But they are often caught on such stuff as a gob of chicken liver which clearly doesn't even look a little bit like a fish. A live night crawler will produce, especially if dancing below a slip-bobber, and cray/crawfish too will be found in their list of good foods to eat. However, the overwhelming volume of food they ingest involve the live fish that are found where they swim. We also catch them on chunks of dead bait as well as popped up dead baits.

So if your lake or river has shad, go with them. If herring are the main forage base, they will work best. Just about every lake and reservoir in America has one kind of shiner or another swimming in its waters so, for sure, they will produce.

There are some states that do not allow use of bait fish that are not commonly found in the water being fished. So don't use live carp if not legal to do so. And don't use baby crappie if your state has a size limit on them. Do not bring in any fish that you netted elsewhere like chub, fallfish, suckers, and the like, if it isn't allowed, so check your state's rule book, please, before bringing anything to the water.

## Time of Day

The best time to catch hybrid bass is anytime you can get out on the water, because they often feed at wildly varying times. But if you have to protect your job or marriage, you may need to select some "prime" times to seek out your fish. So try these options:

## Early Morning or Evening

And, sure, everyone says that about nearly all kinds of fish, so that said, let's dig deeper. Especially in the summer or in waters that are very warm much of the year, it often is better when the water is coolest on top, and that means early morning or late evening, plain and simple. But let's go even more into depth about this.

## "Magic Hour"

While hybrid bass are often seen chasing bait and get caught near the top just after sunrise and a bit before sunset, "Magic Hour" is quite specific. We will talk a bit later about how to, and why to "double-anchor" so for now, let's just say that double-anchoring is what I want you to do. Set your boat over a slope of deep water bottom, even if a dissolved oxygen problem is present, making the lower 50-80% of the water stone dead void of oxygen.

Hybrid bass will range through the deepest parts of your venue, chasing bait or just getting ready to do so as it approaches the time that darkness is nearing. Pick a late afternoon in the summer, and get set up a little more than two full hours before total dead darkness. Whatever style you select, plug or bucktail casting blindly, swinging a big and shiny streamer fly on your light wand, or bait fishing, like I do, get ready, 'cause they are coming, any minute!

Let's say it gets totally black of night dark where you are, at, for example, 8:30 p.m. Be comfortably positioned by 5 or 5:30. Humor yourself by catching such annoying other fish present like bass and crappie, maybe pike too. But somewhere between 90 and 120 minutes before it gets black out, there will be Rockets on the move. The action generally stops around thirty minutes before it darkens completely. I don't know, maybe they rest for a while before feeding again after dark. But in those 60 to 90 minutes before the 30 minutes before dark, listen up and soon enough, the sound of a drag or two or three will get you totally nuts because that is "Magic Hour." This term was invented by a Party Boat Captain in New Jersey named Mic Vassallo for night whiting fishing. They are but a memory now, so I stole the term and adapted it to use on hybrid bass.

## Late Night

Be careful here, because there are many places that it is either illegal or downright dangerous to fish at night. Ever since 9/11, lots of waters were closed just before dark to protect against sabotage. So don't fish where you cannot do so. And if legal, still exercise extreme caution, especially if alone. Trying to get your car/truck and trailer backed up to the ramp at night time isn't a pretty sight, and you could also be somewhere that crooks prowl.

But if it's both safe and legal, by all means, try to fish at night. Some guys troll and still others fish bait. A legally lit boat, maybe with lanterns on, could bring baitfish near the top and where baitfish are, hybrid are sure to follow.

Remember, safety first. Have a first aid kit with you and do try to not do this alone.

## Vibration Time

I thought that I made this term up as well as the explanation for it, but since coining the term, several more knowledgeable folks told me that it existed already, and had a legitimate explanation. So let me at least tell you about Vibration Time, which relates to Lateral Line Time.

All fish have a lateral line that runs from head to tail. And as they feel a vibration in the water, they often get jarred into action. At times, the action is to swim far away in fear. Other times though, this signals the time to tie on the feed bag.

When baitfish are being chased, they give off a vibration that creates interest very far off. And when a school of marauding fish is doing the chasing, they make for even stronger vibrations underwater.

So, if you get a bite, prepare for a Vibration Time attack, because when one fish is feeding, that signals the time for other fish to get into the swing of things. The unwanted silence of the day gets jarred by the sound of drag. And then another line or two gets yanked. You could have several lines out, far from the boat, and one or two straight down. Sure, two near each other simply signals that two feeding fish bit. But I have had countless double strikes, a second or two apart, on two lines that are 100 feet away from each other. That second bite was a Vibration bite, caused by the fish's lateral line.

## Solunar Time

I never did get the technical reason for this. It relates, somehow or another, to the way that the moon and sun line up. However, when they line up correctly, and if no new wind or sudden barometer change occurs, "Solunar Time" often means it's time to get serious.

I have fished in the middle of the day in the center of summer, and when Solunar time is present, somehow the fish just get plain old hungry.

Nearly every good fishing magazine lists "best times to fish." These times are, I believe, related directly to Solunar times. There are four peak periods as a rule. Two occur before noon and two after. Both before and after, there are "Major" periods and "Minor" periods. Say, for example, the first half of the day shows a 1 a.m. Major and a 7 a.m. Minor. And then the second half has a 1:30 p.m. Major and a 7:30 p.m. Minor. Each period, minor or major, start at the time shown. The majors run for 90 to 120 minutes, and the minor ones only last 30 minutes. So if your table shows a Major peak of noon, get set and ready by 11 a.m. because from noon on, for 90 minutes or so, you could be in on some red hot action, summertime or not.

## Time of Year

This one really varies, depending on how far south you are fishing. In some of the deep-south lakes, the fishing is often best as winter breaks into spring. In such states, the action often slows down to a crawl in the middle of a hot summer day. But even in the deepest parts of the south, action can be found, especially while trolling deep.

For certain, the fish need to be warmer than cold so forget about ice fishing. As pointed out elsewhere, I even offered a free book to anyone catching a hybrid through the ice in New Jersey, and no one has submitted such proof. Yes, such catches do occur, but not often.

So just let your locale determine when you should give it a try. Clearly, get out early in the year in any event because one never knows when the hybrid will turn on. You may not get to see a feeding frenzy, but that doesn't mean that they won't bite.

*Hybrids like warmer water, but check out the snow behind
Brady Jenkins at Willard Bay, Utah.*

# Where

Are you fishing in the south, south-central, or more north? And is your site a river or still water? These often call for large changes depending on your answer.

Come spring, just about everywhere, hybrid bass tend to seek out moving water. Sure, river fish are always in such water, but even they chug further upstream in an attempt at spawning, because their biological clock says it is time to breed. And because they cannot breed (being "hybrid"), about the only thing left to do is eat, so get out in the spring and fish in moving or nearby to moving water.

If your reservoir has a power facility and/or a dam, you should fish just below the outfall. Not only will the fish make an attempt at climbing up, they will also be more comfortable in the warmer discharged water. Even with no such power plant, when a river or stream dumps into a lake, get thee to that connection because that may be where the fish will "stage" and get ready to move upstream from. As the waters warm a bit, the fish might already be up the creek and since they don't have a "paddle" (sorry, I get humor whenever possible), you may as well try to catch some at this area.

Back-up waters found in rivers are always good spots. Hybrid are found in such holes and either rest or simply lay there in hiding, waiting for a freebie to drift past. Such holes are closest to shore and you can easily locate them in normal height conditions by seeing a kind of reverse swirl on top of the water. And the good thing is that, once located and remembered, you should be able to head back to these spots time after time and catch a hiding hybrid bass or two.

And there are the guys who like to catch them from shore, like my friend Bruce Condello. He goes after his fish directly from the shore, as you will see when you get to the "Midword" he wrote herein.

Generally speaking, hybrid bass are found in deep, open water when it is warm, away from largemouth bass. However in cool times, they may also be near shore where the water is a tad warmer.

## Rods, Reels, and Line

Spinning rods are generally preferred because their open faced reels offer such a particularly wonderful sound when a Rocket launches itself. But so-called "spin-cast" models, containing "closed-face" reels (commonly found in the south) really aren't a very good option, for one very simple reason... you are fishing "blind!"

Well, I do remember using such an outfit that I had won as a prize a lot of years ago. I was fishing for carp from the shoreline of the Delaware River when a beast took my cooked corn meal offering. My "Mr. Man" (I call all carp "Mr. Man" because of the way that they pull like a man, even if they are females) ran off drag. And then the fish couldn't take any more line out. That was because it took all the line, straight down to the knot, but I couldn't see what had taken place because the "closed-face" covered the spool. My friend Ron Bern and I boarded my beached eight foot boat and followed the fish downstream and I finally caught up to it and bested the 10 pound carp, then releasing it.

So unless you have a closed-face reel with an unlimited volume of line on the spool, or somehow or another, know by instinct when the bare spool is about to show its dark and ugly face, forget fishing for hybrid bass with such an outfit. Save it for largemouths.

Don't buy the cheapest reel you can find, either. Get help here and spend more money rather than less to ensure having a reel that will stand up to the pressure of a hybrid bass run. I was given a new reel back in the 70's. The guy told me that it was the prototype of the first reel made that had an automatic triggering device which opened the reel for casting. And then I got a hit with it off of a pier in Aruba. The reel exploded, with bale going this way, and trigger that way. Buy good, well known reels, or go fish for 10 inch trout.

Bait casting outfits work fine, especially the longer ones that can handle a hybrid's powerful run better than little skinny ones. A stiff action rod may be best, but with bait casting reels, you don't usually get the great sound of a spinning reel, nor the smooth drag unless you paid a bundle. And it can "backlash," making you a very, very unhappy camper indeed.

Fly rods? Yes, for sure, try it if you dare. We will have more on this later on and if you have such skills, by all means, give it a go. Just remember to keep your knuckles out of the way as the reel is revolving backwards in a wild run, or else wear gloves.

Whatever rod, your reel needs to run line off smooth and quick or else prepare to tie on a new rig, because your line will be broken in an instant.

And as for line, change it often and keep your spool filled nearly to the tippety top. Use good line, not junk, and forget about that non-stretch stuff. I was given a spool to field-test and got a great bite. Line tore off as I picked up the outfit and accidentally got the last joint of my right middle finger under the line. And then the line cut so deeply into that joint that I darn-near could see my knee through it (well, a little lie, maybe). Trust me, you can hear and see a hybrid bite on plain old monofilament. You really don't need to use the non-stretch stuff. Save it for fish that don't hit so hard and fast.

## Rigs, Including Floats & Knots

The best rig is one that you tie yourself. Don't buy store-bought ones. Don't use plastic-wrapped snelled hooks because they are almost always tied on too heavy a monofilament and create more trouble than they are worth.

And when it comes to knots, you can go become a Boy Scout or maybe join the Navy and ask to be a Boatswain's Mate. Either of these positions could get you to learn fancy knots. And, yes, you can pick up a knot-tying booklet. Ande line puts one out but in truth, all you need is one knot when you aren't worrying about one slipping out on the non-stretch stuff.

**Knots.** A plain and simple four turn clinch knot is the easiest and close to the strongest you can tie. Get anything you can find, maybe on the internet, and practice tying a clinch knot. Make sure you bring it up as tightly as possible to avoid it opening. A clinch knot that isn't tightly pulled could result in what folks call "curly-cues," as the end of your line looks like a little piggy's tail, because it wasn't closed tight. Yes, an "Improved clinch" tied correctly is better yet, but it is also far easier to tie poorly, resulting in that very embarrassing pig-tail curly-cue.

**Suspended.** The easiest and maybe the best "rig" to use involves cutting off three plus feet of mono off of your reel. Set it aside but tie a non-offset hook, maybe the #6 Mustad model 3906 I favor, to one end. And to the other end, tie on a dark barrel swivel, the second or third smallest size you can find. Now slip an egg sinker onto your main line, say ½ to a full ounce, depending on how big a baitfish you will use, and tie your main line onto the barrel swivel. You will be "rigged" with a sinker that can freely slide up your main line as a fish strikes at the baited hook.

Drop down part-way to the bottom with one line, and maybe further with another, and stick one dead at bottom, and wait to see which one gets more bites and then bring them all to the same depth. You can only do this successfully when fishing from a boat with two anchors, one fore and one aft, as we will shortly discuss. Separate each line well from the other to help in avoiding tangles as an angry fish swims away.

**Floats.** Second style involves the use of a slip-bobber (a/k/a slider-float). Any good one will come in a baggie that has instructions which will tell you how to rig it. Simply though, you will affix a non-moving piece of what appears like sticky dental floss to your line first. This will become a "bobber-stopper." Next comes a hollow red bead, and then your float itself. Beneath the float and just before the top of your barrel swivel will be a ¼ ounce egg sinker. Remember that three plus foot leader above? Have one already set up with your hook already on and tie your main line to the top of the barrel.

Properly rigged, you will have, from bottom to top, 1) hook, 2) leader, 3) barrel swivel bottom, 4) barrel swivel top, 5) egg sinker, 6) float, 7) bead, 8) bobber stopper.

The float will rest on top of the water at any depth you want. Trust me, this is tricky but once you do it, you will remember. The baited hook and sinker will run through the hollow float until it reaches the bead that gets stopped by the bobber-stopper string, and you will be out there, away from the boat, waiting for a strike.

**No rig.** Style number three involves the use of nothing at all other than a plain hook. No float. No sinker. No leader, just the hook. Tie your hook onto your line, bait it with a lively fish of choice like a shad or herring, and cast way out, away from the boat, downwind. Called "live-lined," or "sinker-free," your baitfish will swim freely, attracting anything nearby to visit, and usually, to gobble it up.

## Hooks

STRONG ones, please. A skinny shanked hook may work for crappie, pickerel, and a variety of fish. But a hybrid bass will straighten a light-shanked hook out like a pin in an instant. I always use a Mustad model 3906 hook. This straight-shanked model is thin enough, but still quite strong and is virtually impossible to bend out of shape. Depending on the size of your bait and the fish you seek, go with smaller rather than larger hooks. I usually use a size 6, smaller than most fishermen use, but I've still managed to catch hundreds of hybrid bass from 8-10 pounds on them. If your bait is extra large, or the fish you are after are known to be true beasts, you may want to use a size 4 or even a 2 (larger than 6). Just remember, quality hooks, and with adequately thick shanks.

Last but not least, the hook used for live baitfish needs to be non-offset. A hybrid running away will turn the bait and swallow. If the hook has a curved shank, ala the "beak" model, you stand a good chance at the Rocket turning the hook into the back of the baitfish, double-hooking it, and making it impossible to stick your fish. Offset hooks work well with night crawlers or chicken liver, but not otherwise.

Some folks prefer to use treble hooks and while you will miss less fish with them, it will also be more difficult to practice "Catch & Release" with one. The treble could be swallowed and it would be a bit tougher for the fish to still eat while waiting for the hook to rust out. But still, I remember cleaning a lake trout that had five hook points in it and still managed to eat my shiner. One point was on a size 8 single hook, another on a 1/0 and three were on a size six treble. Half of each point had already rusted away.

Yes, there are countless anglers who swear that a "Circle" hook is best and if you want to go with such a model, feel free. But I still will stick with my #3906.

## Kinds of Lures, Including Flies

Stickbaits, spoons, jigs and flies. But which ones? For the most part, select ones that look like the bait fish that hybrid bass can find in your venue of choice. Make sure to have a floating plug or two that looks like a herring. A floater, because when the fish are boiling on top, you want to place a lure not far away that will float. At times, you only need to turn the handle once or twice to elicit a strike from a nearby Rocket.

Sinking plugs are used for blind casting, but more so, in the next section, while trolling. Spoons are only put into play on the troll, unless you are in fast moving water and can hold them just off bottom on a down-rigger, ala shad fishing.

Jigs are commonly put into play for both blind casting and trolling, but make sure your jig is wider than most to try to emulate the movement of a shad or herring.

Flies are the kinds of lures that may get you nailed more directly into a fish than any other manner of lure. Imagine your size six white streamer, marabou or bucktail-tied, with sparkling mylar tied in for good measure. And picture it as you are about to lift it off the water to start another roll cast when it gets inhaled by a speeding bullet! If that doesn't get your knees knocking, nothing else will, so go take up golf.

Try this, if you dare. Fish with two flies in tandem. You could also use a very small jig at the end of the line with a fly tied in, two feet above it. So, one fly followed by another or a jig with a streamer riding ahead, can often induce two fish to strike, sometimes together.

The vibration caused by fish #1 (see Vibration Time) will trigger a response to lure #2 from fish that might not have eating on their minds at all. Of course, how you deal with trying to best two Rockets going in different directions is strictly up to you. But we should all have such difficult problems.

# Trolling

Trolling really works exceptionally well for folks with mechanical skill. I have little, if any, but still manage to catch a few hybrid bass while pulling two lines behind the boat, one on each corner, with live herring as bait. Sure, the real pros pull a whole gang of lures at a variety of depths. But whenever I even try to put a third outfit into play, I nearly always tangle two or three of them together within a minute of the very first tiny turn the boat takes.

But fellows who have a bunch of rod holders placed in different angles can drag at least a half-dozen live baits or lures behind the boat. And if they have a few downriggers, they can add yet more lines into the game.

So troll if you know how, because it certainly will work. Make sure to vary your speeds because you never know at what speed they will want the bait/lure to be swimming. For sure though, if your rods are in rod holders, have them as deeply in as you can get them. And be certain that your drags are set to release line, or maybe be ready to re-rig after a fish snaps your tight-drag set line in an instant. You may also have to prepare to wave bye-bye to a rod that is yanked skyward out of the holder. It will raise up to the sky a bit but will eventually come down, as the hybrid drags it beneath the surface.

# From Shore

Clearly, guys like Bruce Condello in Kansas and his cousin, and others too, have perfected a system that is so incredibly good that I wonder why I never tried it myself. They fish lures into the wind on specific kinds of days with certain types of conditions, as you will read in Bruce's "Midword." But aside from them, casting flies or plugs from the shore could produce action almost every evening. Still fishing with live or even cut baitfish can also get you into some hybrid bass. And there are many waters, moving or still, in which hybrid seem to really love to eat chicken liver more than nearly anything else. And, no, chicken liver doesn't swim, but still they gobble it up.

# Drifting

Find fish boiling on top and, for sure, don't even dream of anchoring. Instead, drift towards the action after cutting your electric motor and cast into the excitement. Just know though that you can't get more than a rod or two out while drifting, because if you do, and you hook a hybrid, it will turn the boat around in a circle and tangle all the lines up into one incredible to look at mass of mess.

I once watched a hybrid turn a 20 foot aluminum pontoon boat, with the weight of four big guys and two heavy engines on board, completely around and start dragging it the other way. The three other anglers only had one line out each but all four rods wound up tied into a hopeless tangle, as the fish broke off.

# Anchoring

Two anchors should be on board your boat, no matter how small it is, unless you are using a rubber tube, maybe, or a kayak or canoe. Presuming your boat is at least a dozen feet long and not John-boat style, with a bow that can dunk into the drink in a heart-beat, always have two anchors with you.

You see, if you anchor up with only one from the bow and have, say five lines out and you don't even get a bite, the boat will turn this way and that in wind or stillness, and you will be disengaging lines from each other all day long. And with a fish on, a Rocket? Ooh, Nellie, all the lines will become like one, as the fish turns the boat around. **So do have two anchors, please.**

Presuming you are fishing a river or stream, your anchors should be so-called "river anchors," made of single unit construction. Specially made, they have grooves that get you into bottom, but not so deeply that you may have to cut your anchor line to go home. Of course if you are fishing in fast current, be sure your boat has high sides before trying to fish two anchors. And make certain that you are in water that isn't too skinny so that two anchors will block other boats' movement.

Whether river or lake, be certain to have not less than five times the amount of line on each anchor as the depth of the water in which you intend to anchor. If sticking into 50 feet of water at one end of the boat and at 40 on the other end, have at least 200 to 300 feet of good, quality ⅜ inch nylon anchor line, with no knots. A knot will not be good, trust me. It will tangle in the line and seriously impede your ability to lay line out and retrieve it smoothly and evenly.

In still water, put anchor #1 overboard, (a 4-6 pound "Danforth" model) and get it dug into bottom as you back up slowly. Make sure you are tightly dug in and then go back lots more. Most people stop when the first one is in and then put #2 in. That makes it impossible to get each anchor far away from both ends of the boat.

When #1 is dug, again, back way up, go into neutral and put #2 over, trying to get the boat eventually set up with a whole side of the boat facing any breeze that is blowing. Okay, #2 went in and dropped to bottom. Take some slack line from the stuff that is in the back of the boat and head up forward. Grab the slack anchor line #1 and start to pull the boat up towards where #1 is, as you dig #2 in, and then release line from #2. This works far easier if you have another person on board, but on the other hand, they could catch some of your fish too so try to perfect this style alone if you are as selfish as I am.

#2 now also in, just pull enough line on #1 so that each anchor is in bottom and you have at least 50 feet of line out from both ends of the boat. In this manner with both lines now tightly tied to either end, and with little if any slack, you will be in perfect position.

Perfect, so that a hooked fish can be led around the top of an anchor line or under it and around to the other side of the boat. I have caught literally hundreds of hybrid bass that took me from one side of the boat to the other, and, maybe, got wrapped so tightly around an anchor line that I had to break off, maybe, just maybe, twice, ever!

And did I tell you to make sure that the far end of each anchor line is tied tightly into the boat? No? Oh-oh, please do so because when that squiggly end goes into the water, will you ever cuss me out or what? Make sure you have four feet of chain on each anchor to ease in digging in.

## Catch and Release

Far and away, the overwhelming majority of hybrid bass that I catch get released. Do not take this as a lecture to get you cranky if you want to bring one home for a meal from time to time. I do so, but that only involves 5-10 fish yearly out of 100 to 200 that I catch.

You will see some pictures in this book of dead fish. Hey, guides may encourage their customers to catch and release, but still, if the customer wants to bring a few home, the boss is the boss. Some pictures may have been provided of State Record fish, and most will be of dead fish.

But for sure, do try to release nearly every hybrid bass you catch. Even if they swallow your hook, cut the line at the mouth and let it go. Nearly all will survive, unless you make them bleed by trying to dig the ten cent hook out.

There may be a state or two that suggests or even tells you to keep all that you catch until you reach the bag limit. Some folks feel that hybrid bass fight so very hard that some will die, even after being released. But I really feel that this is a very rare occurrence.

## CHAPTER 5

# Rules And Regulations

A s I walk you through the basics, please note that whatever I say, chances are good to excellent that no matter what you read here, things will CHANGE! So if I say that a size or bag limit may apply in your state today, it could be quite different tomorrow.

If you are alone, make sure to have a current list of rules and regulations with you at all times to be current. For sure, you don't want to have a fish on your stringer that is smaller than legal, or have one more than the bag limit either!

Call this a cop-out if you want but when you are writing about a particular fish in an entire country like I'm trying here, take it to the bank that I will either tell you about something that may change later in this very year or worse, that I may make a mistake altogether. And, yes, I do make mistakes, I just need someone else to blame so in this case, it could be you!

Some states limit the number of rods and reels that you can use so, even though I set my little boat up on anchor to look like a battleship, with "guns" pointed this way and that, make sure your state allows use of multiple outfits. And if I tell you that I catch fish while chumming with chunks of dead baitfish, make certain that your state permits chumming, because some don't.

## CHAPTER 6

# Some Basic Stuff

There are many private lakes across America which hold hybrid bass, but since I only wanted to tell you about venues that are open to the public, I didn't write about any of them. But I do list three "Open-To-The-Public" ponds in New Jersey where you can pay a fee and catch some of these fish. Chances are that your state also has such pay-ponds, but again, I have omitted the private lakes because you cannot fish there anyway!

Twenty-nine states actively stock hybrid bass in some of their waters. And at least one or two have stocked them in the past but for one reason or another, have stopped. Still others may have some hybrid bass present in their waters that stumbled in.

Hybrid bass have wanderlust. Being part-striped bass, a fish that once was only found in salt water, I think that many of the current fish feel that they, somehow or another, belong elsewhere, like in the brine! And whenever a hybrid bass can wander, wander many of them do. So if a lake dumps into a river, or vice-versa, the fish may try to escape into the river and follow it downstream or up to reach salt. Every now and then, a hybrid is caught in the Atlantic Ocean and chances are that they are escapees from a lake that drained into a stream which plopped into a river that emptied into the ocean.

*Joe Bauer Jr. holding a Rocket caught at the family pay-pond.*

CHAPTER 7

# The 50 States, Those That DO and Those That DON'T

## ☑ ALABAMA — YES

S ince we are starting at the beginning of the alphabetical list of all 50 states, I guess it's a good thing that we start with one that actually does stock my favorite fish, Alabama. Alabama has an aggressive stocking program for hybrid bass and Doug Darr, Education Director for the Division of Wildlife and Freshwater Fisheries gave me several good pointers. And back in 2002 when I wrote an article about hybrid bass for a nationwide magazine, Joe Addison also shared more details with me.

I suppose that one thing that needs to be known may deal with rod and reel aggregate limit. There are some states that limit the number of outfits that can be used and still others that have no limits. For sure, ice-fishing season limits differ too in such states that offer "hardwater" opportunities. But as for Alabama, at least based on regulations that existed during the 2004-2005 season, only two bodies of water had aggregate rod and reel limits, Weiss Reservoir and Neely Henry Lake. Each only allows three outfits to be used per angler.

Another important regulation to adhere to relates to how many fish an angler can keep, and at what sizes. Once more, make sure

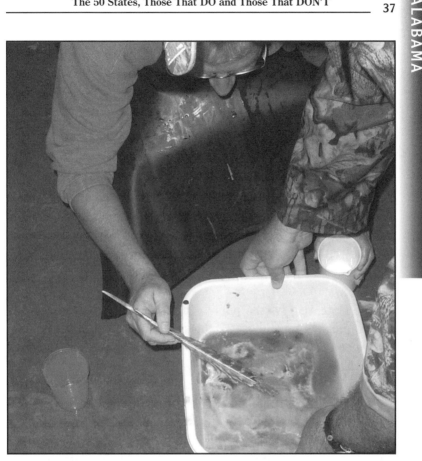

*Bill Starks, Manager of the Marion, Alabama Fish Hatchery,*
*using a feather, to stir eggs and milt together.*

you are current because these things do change, but as of the 2004 season, Weiss Reservoir may be the only water that allows up to 30 fish, white bass, yellow bass, striped bass and/or hybrid bass to be kept with no limit as to size. 30 is also the take-home limit throughout the state but at Lewis Smith Reservoir and Lake Martin, you can only keep a total of two of the bigger foursome of fish noted above.

Let's confuse you further now. Go back to that 30 fish limit again — at ANY other water, instead of two at the waters just noted, or no limit at Weiss, the other waters contain regulations that say that not more than six of your overall catch of the four noted fish can exceed 16 inches.

Thus said, please follow my basic rule instead. If you have hungry folks at home, take the least number of the legal limit you are allowed to take, providing you really can finish eating your catch in a single meal. But if you are like me and just love to catch fish, then, please, please, release just about every one you catch. "Catch and release" is the way I go about my business of fishing for hybrid bass and nearly all will survive to live and eat another day unless you really abuse them before putting them back.

Alabama has 47 stocked reservoirs that exceed 500 acres in size and they cover 551,200 acres overall. We cannot very well discuss every lake that has hybrid bass in them, but let's talk about a few that are worth a visit.

The state also has 23 public state park lakes and upwards of 77,000 miles of moving water, much of which containing one kind of striper or another. While some have white bass and still others, especially those near saltwater, have true strain striped bass, let's stick with those that have hybrid bass.

Depending on fall sampling which allows the state to determine hybrid bass survival and growth rates, the state will put more or less in, based on what they discover each autumn. But a good guesstimate would be that 600,000 to 700,000 "stripes" are stocked statewide each year.

Some of the public lakes get fish yearly, as well as the bigger bodies of water such as reservoirs on the Coosa, Alabama, Mobile, and the Warrior River systems. Other large stockings have been made in the Tombigbee and Tennessee River areas. The Mobile Delta also receives plenty of hybrid bass stockings.

It should be noted that while most 'Bama residents call them "Stripes," "hybrids" or "sunshine bass," Joe Addison told me that "die hard" bass anglers often refer to them in a far different manner, meaning they use some of the words I learned in Brooklyn.

Doug Darr said that open reservoir anglers prefer to catch their hybrid bass while the fish are schooling. "Schooling" hybrid bass present a peculiar problem to most freshwater anglers.

You see, most have never seen such an exhibit. And most will do the most unusual things when they see such a sight. Such things include but are not limited to freaking out in excitement because when Rockets school they are not there to learn anything, rather, they are there to tear up as many bait fish as they possibly can.

Little fish swim high to get away and birds swoop down to eat any that the hybrid bass miss. So if you ever see schooling hybrid bass in Alabama, as we do in all of the other states that contain them, do try to avoid having a heart attack and just go about your business of trying to hook up with them.

Mr. Darr added that a preferred alternate to sight fishing for schooling fish would include use of swimming lures and jigs as well as live bait. The tailwaters of the upstream impoundments offer excellent opportunities.

## 🐟 ALASKA — NO

Well, as you might have guessed, Alaska's waters are just too doggone cold most of the year to satisfy the needs of hybrid bass. Yes, some might survive a winter in a deep lake, but not many at that.

In fact, the state told me that there are NO bass of any kind in Alaska, and it is illegal by statute to put any bass in her waters. Rob Bentz, Deputy Director of its Division of Sportfish, provided this information. A statute passed in 2003 threatens everything but loss of all fishing rights for life if anyone brings such a critter in.

So if you want to fish in Alaska, try for halibut, ling-cod, salmon, trout, and the like as I did several times. No, they aren't hybrid bass, but Alaska's waters still offer wonderful fishing, salt and fresh alike.

## 🐟 ARIZONA — NO

Fisheries Chief Lawrence M. Riley wrote about hybrid bass to say that "their reputation as excellent fighters and a great catch certainly precedes them, and I understand your enthusiasm." But Arizona still has opted to not add these fish to any of its waters. My guess is that if you are a resident of that pretty state, a letter-writing campaign might get them to re-think things because the Chief himself has heard how fine a fish they are.

Meanwhile, Arizona's residents and visitors will have to settle with catching true-strain stripers that have existed in some of its waters going as far back as the year 1970 or so. Initial stocking went into both lakes Mead and Powell. I hired a guide to put me into stripers at Lake Mead some time back and sure enough caught a whole mess of them. But did they fight, pound for pounds, like hybrid bass do? Oh my goodness, not even close, no indeed.

Chief Riley added that stripers have spread into interior Arizona over the years and are currently also found at lakes Mohave and Havasu, plus parts of the Colorado River downstream of Lake Havasu. They are also now found in central Arizona at Lake Pleasant near Phoenix and this lake houses the only population of white bass in the state. Yellow bass can be found at the chain of lakes that are at the Salt River, east of Phoenix.

# ☑ ARKANSAS — YES

Lots of people stepped up to the plate and offered help to me from Arkansas. Among them was Brett Hobbs, Fisheries Biologist with the state out of Hot Springs. Carl Perrin at district 10 was another very helpful state employee.

And I also got plenty of assistance from Jimmy Johnson, a guide who specializes in hybrid bass fishing on DeGray Lake, one of the best Rocket lakes in America. You can reach Jimmy at 1-501-847-4961. Check out his web site at www.tri-lakesguide.com too. Lastly, the internet presents yet more learning opportunities so check that out as well. And here's what I learned and can share.

Perhaps the two most popular hybrid bass waters in Arkansas are the 31,500 acre lake, Greers Ferry in Heber Springs and DeGray Lakes. Each is an Army Corp. of Engineers reservoir. Both lakes produce double-digit hybrid bass annually. And in the north-central part of the state, 22,000 acre Lake Norfolk also receives hybrids on a regular basis. We will talk about this last lake in Missouri too because it is also present there.

*Guide Jimmy Johnson with matched pair of 12 lb. Hybrids —*
*DeGray Lake, Arkansas, on live shad.*

DeGray, in southwest Arkansas, gets 4-8 fingerlings stocked per acre each year, with the variation depending on available stock. When put in, the fish measure an average of two inches. DeGray started getting stockings of hybrids back in the early 70's when several thousand went in. This lake covers 13,400 acres.

In 1976, Greers Ferry's nursery pond got a whopping 1.1 million fry put in that were obtained from Georgia. Half of them reached fingerling size and were added into the main lake later on.

Hybrid bass are commonly caught on live bait. The top two offerings are large shiners or small shad. Topwater plugs, spoons, and bucktail jigs all produce action. Mr. Hobbs said that trolling deep diving jerkbaits and other diving plugs will produce strikes. Topwater action occurs in summer and early fall. Try early mornings or cloudy days.

Arkansas raises both true-strain and hybrid stripers at their facility at the Andrew Hulsey State Fish Hatchery in Hot Springs. Arkansas hybrids are usually a cross of a female striper and a male white bass but as you will learn in this book, many of them are reared with the mix of a male striper and a female white, called a "Reciprocal Cross" by some.

Among the other state waters that receive goodly hybrid bass stockings are:
- Horseshoe Lake in Crittenden County
- DeQueen Lake in Sevier County
- Storm Creek Lake in Phillips County
- Little River below Lake Millwood.

There are plenty more on the list though, well over a dozen other lakes. Storm Creek, which is in the St. Francis National Forest north of West Helena, is a little lake (at least small for Arkansas). This lake is only 420 acres in size.

One of the Arkansas Sportsman articles I found on the "net" quoted writer Jim Spencer when he fished for hybrid bass on yet another lake, Hamilton by name. He said that "It felt like I'd foul-hooked a small submarine." And I can only add, you betcha!

Several hybrid bass have been caught in Arkansas that (be still, my knocking knees) hit or exceeded 20 pounds! Among which was the 21 pound beast that came out of DeGray Lake in 1989. But even better was the fish that held the state record, caught at Greers Ferry Lake in April of 1997 by Jerald Shaum of Shirley, Arkansas. It weighed 27 pounds, 5 ounces. And by now, a new World Record may have been certified in Arkansas because Frank

Talbert Jr. caught a 29 lb 1 oz monster in Bull Shoals Lake in February of 2004!

Fish and Game Commission's Keith Sutton wrote an article for the Arkansas Sportsman Magazine which said that the state hybrid bass record was broken 24 times over the twelve year period beginning with a little 1.2 pounder back in 1976. The overwhelming majority of these came from DeGray.

And here's a direct quote from his article-with additional comment from me being completely unnecessary: "I was left breathless in the wake of the frenzied battle on DeGray Lake."

Beaver Lake, in northwest Arkansas, near Rogers, is a 28,800 acre lake that is deep, clear and rocky. It holds both true-strain stripers and hybrid bass. Yet another body of water with both fish is the 34,300 chunk called Lake Dardanelle near Russelville.

Different catch limits exist on the lakes in Arkansas, and again, since things change, don't be sure that what I am about to tell you is correct — instead, consult your compendium. At one time, it was six fish per angler at DeGray and Greers Ferry with half that being allowed to go home out of Lake Norfolk.

## 🚫 CALIFORNIA — NO

And, yes, the answer is no, even though California has a perfect climate for hybrid bass and even has a private hatchery that rears hybrid bass in it. In fact, the State of Oregon purchases the small hybrid bass that they stock from this California-based hatchery!

Sure, California offers wonderful salt water fishing (I've done well there several times with everything from halibut to barracuda). It is very well known for its gigantic largemouth bass and huge rainbow trout. But who knows, maybe one day they will introduce their residents to hybrid bass and only then will the state really understand what kind of spectacular fish they have added.

California offers her residents a shot at white bass in one venue and numerous waters hold true strain stripers but, golly gee, no Rockets. Maybe one day, they will join in on the fun and become the 30th state that stocks wipers.

# ☑ COLORADO — YES

Trout? Oh my, yes indeed, Colorado has many varieties of trout swimming around in its wonderfully clear and cool mountain streams. But until I looked on a map and saw that the state is situated right in the middle part of the 48 states, I always pictured it as being more to the north, and didn't you too?

Yes, clearly, Colorado is better known for its super trout action, be they rainbow, cutthroat, brown, or brook. And don't forget the biggest trout of all, lakers, and the hybrid version, splake, which is a cross between a lake trout and a brookie.

Colorado also has several other hybrids: tiger muskies (northern pike and muskellunge cross), and saugeye, the hybrid of a walleye and a sauger. But my favorite is the hybrid bass, as you may have figured out by now, so let's talk about them.

Robin Knox, Manager of the Colorado Sport Fishing Program told me that the top hybrid lures used include an assortment of crankbaits, plus jigs, spinner baits and bass assassins. He favors sunrise through the next two hours for top action, but also feels that the two hours before sunset until sunset itself are quite good.

One of the biggest hybrid bass caught in the whole country came out of Pueblo Reservoir in Colorado, a 26 lb. 15 ounce monster.

I was told that the state began stocking hybrid bass back in 1981 by Gregory W. Gerlich. He was the Fisheries Biologist in the S. Park Area with the state when he wrote to me in 2002. Greg said that the state's eastern plains impoundments offer the best chance at catching hybrid bass. He said (what everyone else does who has seen their fighting skill), that they are a fantastic sportfish species.

ColoradoFisherman.com describes the fish as "schooling fish that can be found 'busting' prey fish on the surface during the summer." They suggest casting shad imitations or other lures at the breaking fish and holding on tight. Trolling is another suggested style.

Robin Knox sent me a 25 page study of all of the hybrid bass that Colorado has made available to their anglers since the program started back in 1981 and, the numbers really boggle one's mind. I

*Robin Knox, Colorado Sportfish Program Manager sent in this picture. One of their guys stocking a lake with lots of fingerling-sized hybrids.*

got a little cross-eyed trying to produce enough representative data for you regarding their program and I hope that I got it right.

Some years had less fish stocked than others, no doubt caused by a lack of availability of either small fish or funds, as with the year 2002. Still, 1,500,000 small fry went into a variety of lakes that year.

The program began with the stocking of three bodies of water and all three remain favorites to this day with the state and its fishermen. They include Bonny Reservoir which got the massive number of 373,000 3/4 inch fish that year.

Stockings continued there with most recent numbers including 18,000 plus one inch fish in 2000, 35,000 one inchers and 200,000 small fry in 2001, and 200,000 fry in each of 2003 and 2004.

John Martin Reservoir got 13,281 babies that averaged close to two inches in 1981, and later on, 46,000 one inch fish in 2000 as well as 300,000 fry. Next year, it got 110,000 1 plus inch fish and 600,000 fry, a huge number indeed. In 2003 200,000 fry went in, and the largest stocking in 2004 went into John Martin, 900,000 little fry!

Nee Noshe was the third reservoir that was tested with hybrid bass in 1981 when 5,100 fish that were nearly two inches long were stocked. And in the years 2000, 2001, 2003, and 2004, yet 1,100,000 more fry got stocked. 25,000 one inch plus fish also were added in 2001.

Among the other lakes that received exceedingly large stockings of hybrid bass in the years starting with 2000 include Adobe Creek, Henry Lake, Jackson Reservoir, Nee Gronde Reservoir, and North Sterling Reservoir.

In the year 2004 alone, 30 separate stockings of hybrid bass took place in Colorado and for sure, that means that this state really takes its hybrid bass fishery serious!

## ⊘ CONNECTICUT — NO

Hey, I've written an entire book about the great fishing that can be found in Connecticut ("Gone Fishin' ... The 75 Best Waters in Connecticut"). But the state has opted to not add hybrid bass in any of its waters. The state has a whole shoreline that offers residents full access to many thousands of true strain striped bass. And three major rivers crank up into the state with loads of stripers chugging up each winter to hold over and attempt to spawn.

These are the reason given for not putting hybrid bass into Connecticut but, hey, New Jersey has the very same striper situation and still puts lots of hybrid bass into some selected waters. Maybe Connecticut will join in one day? I hope so.

# ☑ DELAWARE — YES

Lum's Pond, plain and simple. If you want to catch a hybrid bass in Delaware, this is the place to go.

Sure, the state has many miles of shoreline which offer residents and visitors a fine opportunity to catch true-strain striped bass, but still, many prefer hybrids. They don't grow as big as striped bass do but, pound for pound (sorry, striper nuts), a five pound hybrid can tow a 10 pound true strain behind it without knowing that anything is attached. You will see me write a variation or two of this elsewhere in the book, because I really do believe it to be so.

Back in 1990, Earl Blevins of Newark, Delaware established the state record with his 13 pound, 13½ ounce beauty at the lake. Landbigfish.com's site showed a photo of a 7.10 pounder nailed by an angler on 4/9/02 on a bonewhite SuperSpook Jr., lure. A chilly and wet rain was falling that evening as the angler caught his fish while wading but my guess is that he was plenty warm for a while thereafter.

Lum's Pond is situated near the town of Glasgow, just north of the C&D Canal.

Fisheries Biologist Catherine C. Martin reported the state beginning its hybrid stocking in 1982 after first putting a mess of landlocked alewife herring in, bought at Lake Hopatcong in New Jersey. 1,000 to 1,500 hybrids, which averaged a half-a-foot, went in yearly for over 10 years.

A serious supply and demand situation exists at the lake, and the state has monitored things quite well. You see, at times, the hybrid eat most the food in the lake making it tough for largemouth bass anglers to be happy. So they buy herring from time to time to help supply forage and some years, the state skips a hybrid bass stocking. Natural herring reproduction has occurred which certainly helps.

Back in 2002, Ms. Martin also told me that the lake is 189 acres, near Newark, De., and stockings generally take place each fall. The lake is a state park and is subject to a user fee in season. Boats and canoes can be rented and many other facilities are available such as trails, campsites, a nature center and fishing piers. So this is a place to enjoy for the whole family.

Most citation-size fish, (5 pounds, or 22 inches for the live-release program) are caught in April or May and later, in October and November. Cooler water temperatures are preferred and they tend to congregate in the deepest portions of the pond in the summer.

The prevailing limits as we went to print allowed an angler to keep two fish if they reach or exceed 15 inches in length. Of course many anglers view these fish as too precious to keep for a meal and that may be why the state has its own catch and release citations.

For more information about the park, call the office, 302-368-6989. A special kid's fishing tournament is held by the state here in June and for details, call 302-739-3440.

Many of the states in the country have true strain stripers and use that as a reason to keep hybrid bass out, feeling that the fish might confuse anglers. There was even a case some time ago in which a judge allowed an angler to escape a fine when he said that he thought he had caught a hybrid instead of a striper. (You have to be nearly blind to not see the difference, and even if you cannot see, you sure can feel the difference in the quality of their respective fights.)

But such states as Delaware, Pennsylvania and New Jersey have both fish and, somehow or another, things have worked out just fine. So, other states, what's up with you, huh?

## ☑ FLORIDA — YES

And what better name could this wonderful state have given to my favorite beast than "Sunshine?" After all, Florida truly is "The Sunshine State," right? In fact though, when Florida first starting stocking some of its water with hybrid bass in the 70's, they were the cross-breeds of female striped bass and male white bass, obtained from South Carolina, and they were to be called Palmetto bass in Florida.

But then as Florida developed their own hybrids, they did so by using the roe of a female white bass and the sperm of a male

*Florida angler with a real nice hybrid, nailed below the Jim Woodruff Dam, courtesy of Phil Chapman, FI F&WCC*

striper, the opposite of the more typical cross still stocked in many states. And Florida then called this creation "Sunshine" bass. Florida felt that the male striper and female white cross would be easier to raise based on timing factors and brood stock availability.

Florida gives their baby fish a jump start at survival by injecting the selected adults with hormones before removing roe and sperm and then they actually mix the stuff together by hand.

Eggs are aerated in special containers called MacDonald jars until they hatch.

I received lots of help back in 2002 from James Estes, Chief of the Bureau of Fisheries Resources, and then still more late in 2004 from Phil Chapman, Fisheries Biologist with the Florida Fish & Wildlife Conservation Commission out of Lakeland, Fl. Phil was also good enough to ask biologists Rick Stout at the Richloam Hatchery in Webster and Dave Yeager of the Blackwater Hatchery in Holt, Fl., to provide me with stocking data.

The bottom line of all this is that Florida raises and stocks an average of 2,000,000 hybrid bass each year in a wide range of waters, both rivers and lakes alike. The fish average an inch to two inches and because they aren't what are considered "fry" elsewhere (because they are a bit bigger), they stand a better chance at survival than the little guys.

According to Phil Chapman, a wide variety of baits and lures are hit from time to time by sunshine bass. Artificial lures such as shad-imitating crank-baits, twitchbaits and surface plugs in chrome and other light colors work. You will be trying to match the shad that make up the main diet of these magnificent fish.

When in murky water, try a plug with an internal noise maker (you know of a few, I'm sure, that-RATTLE-got it?) Plastic grubs and bucktail jigs also produce, in white and chartreuse.

Fly guys get their arms jolted to the elbow when they stick back at a hybrid that inhaled their white streamer. Try a deceiver, Clouser, or small bunker-type fly. A touch of mylar couldn't hurt either.

When sunshine bass are pounding into schools of shad up on top (wait, let me just think about that for a moment and shudder a bit), try a surface fly or popper. A fast retrieve will work when they are on top, and there is no such thing as too fast then.

And while these fish sure hit lures, they are far from overly selective. You can catch them on a bobber rig with live shiner hung a few feet below. Live shad will work even better but don't stop there. A fat night crawler will produce serious action but now for the silliest bait of all, chicken liver! Yup, chicken liver, far from being a natural bait, but a hunk on bottom may be the best hybrid attractor of all. Just watch out for catfish action though, and if your venue has turtles, you may have to forget the liver deal.

Trolling produces wonderful action but do make sure your drag is open if you aren't holding onto your rod. If it is in a rod holder with tight drag, prepare to watch the top half of your rod get busted off, or at least your line broken. Out in the ocean, this tends to be called "hooking a snapper," and a hybrid snapping your line sure sounds like that.

Early mornings or late afternoons are generally the top times to catch hybrid bass in most states but don't be surprised if you see a mid-day feeding frenzy.

In the stocking year from 2003 to 2004, a total of 24 separate bodies of water in 10 counties received hybrid bass, statewide. And the year before, 29 waters got the little critters into nine counties.

The fish are placed in waters ranging to the northwest at Pensacola on the Panhandle, all the way down to the southeast at lower West Palm Beach/Lantana into Lake Osborne.

While hybrid bass handle heat far better than true-strain striped bass, they still do not have a terribly long life expectancy because it gets tough for them to handle exceedingly warm water. A typical life span of the fish is 3-5 years but don't worry, they grow very quickly and can reach double figures in ease. And elsewhere in this book you will read that hybrids cannot manage to survive in excessively cold water very well at all.

Florida has selected the waters to stock with hybrid bass quite carefully. They were developed to survive in warm freshwater temperatures and to take advantage of abundant shad forage wherever stocked.

Although most stockings involve the 1-2 inchers noted above, 15,000 to 20,000 larger fish are raised before being put into waters that take more pressure. As a general rule of thumb, most of the larger fish (8-9 inches long) are put into urban fishing ponds and FWC impoundments in the Panhandle. And while you think that a nine inch fish is rather puny, a kid tussling with a nine incher may think that she has a whale on!

Here are what the state itself considered to be the top waters for the year 2004. Chances are good to excellent that each area will remain hot for years to come, while still others will be added later on.

1)-Up at Apalachicola River/Seminole Lake, on the Gulf, the three state record fish that make up this super fish all came out of this river/lake system. At least as of the end of 2004, the heaviest true-strain striped bass was nailed, weighing 42.25 pounds, and the largest white bass, at 4.69 pounds was taken. And the biggest hybrid, a 16.31 pounder, was bested by Thomas R. Elder of Grande Ridge, Fl. at the lake.

200,000 hybrid bass are stocked into Lake Seminole by the state of Georgia, which we will be talking about soon. The lake borders the two states and be careful to obey what are probably special regulations that prevail, based on where you fish as well as where you launch from.

The lake is 35,000 acres in size and is the headwater of the Apalachicola River, at Gadsden and Jackson Counties. State information advises that sunshine bass congregate along the old river channels and the lower lake near the dam during fall and winter. They then migrate up the Chattahoochee and Flint rivers during the spring.

A good Apalachicola River area to try in the spring would be below the Jim Woodruff Dam near Chattahoochee. Come summer, some areas are closed to fishing so make sure you understand all regulations. During fall and winter, other prime areas range from the dam in the river to the coast. A river hot spot would be right below the dam during spring as sunshine bass wait to pick off an easy meal.

2)-The St. Johns River, on the Atlantic Coast. While hybrid bass don't live too terribly long because of warm water, this river presents a chance at longer survival due to cooler and better aerated waters.

The river gets loads of true-strain stripers and had received sunshine bass in large numbers until late in the 90's. Some still are present, and in particular, quite a few from 5-7 pounds. Migrants from the Oklawaha River are also present in the St. Johns.

Try for them at the mouth of Lake Monroe, especially at the RR trestle and the I-4 Bridge pilings. A few other good areas would include the I95 Shands Bridge in Green Cove Springs and other bridges in Jacksonville. Croaker Hole presents cooler water to both hybrid and true-strain stripers.

Since this area has hybrids, whites, and true-stripers, please make sure you can identify each but, as of 2004, the state made things a bit easy by lumping all into the same "catch and keep" total.

3)-Choctawhatchee River. Moving water & hybrid bass ... what a combination! The fish that I catch in still water fight like no other beast around. Having never caught one that was raised by fighting current to survive, I can only imagine how much stronger they must be. Wow!

The river receives alternate year stockings of striped bass and hybrid bass. The main fishery is in the lower river, between State Road 20 and Choctawhatchee Bay, in Walton and Washington counties. The best action takes place during fall and winter. True-strain stripers can be found each summer around coolwater discharges at tributaries.

4)-Escambia River. Here's another river that should get alternate year stockings of sunshine and true strain fish. Until 1999, it had received annual stockings of hybrid bass and then in 2003, 500,000 fingerlings were put in.

The river itself and the Escambia Bay, in Escambia and Santa Rosa counties, offer some hybrid beasts that exceed 10 pounds!

Check out the lower 10 miles of the river and upper bay during fall and winter for best action. Sunshines make a small upriver run during the spring, I suppose, simulating a spawning run but to date, no natural hybrid spawnings have been recorded in Florida.

5)-Eagle Lake is a little, itty bitty water compared to others, but still Florida feels that it really is a fine place to try. My guess is that one reason may be that kids will have relatively easy access. This Fish Management Area is a 200 acre reclaimed phosphate pit in Hamilton County and it gets a whopping 50 to 100 sunshine bass per acre.

The lake has a large forage base of shad and as a result, hybrid bass can grow here to 6 or 7 pounds in as little as two years. There are deep cuts and narrow cuts between the fingers, where sand bars drop off quickly into deep water. Best time to fish Eagle Lake is during fall and winter. Try a diving plug like a Thin-Fin, in shad finish, and hold on!

6)-Edward Medard Lake. Here's another reclaimed set of old phosphate pits that the state puts 100 sunshine bass into yearly per acre. This number is as much as 10 times the average per acre stocking that is done in many other places.

Located in Hillsborough County, stocking here just began in earnest recently but some two year old fish have already been caught that hit six pounds.

7)-Lake Osborne and Lake Ida are two bodies that run into each other. A joint can be found off 6th Street in Lake Worth, just to the west of Route 95. This is the southernmost place that gets hybrid bass in Florida, I suppose because the waters from here on down may get too warm to sustain life as they heat up.

Although it's situated in Palm Beach County, where most anglers in the area prefer the abundant saltwater action available only a mile or two to the east, this connected place still is very popular. In fact, you can often see a load of those glitzy sparkle-plenty bass boats on the lakes. They are usually not after sunshine bass though, and instead are casting into the weeds and wood at both shores for largemouth bass.

You may be able to tell when a Lake Osborne largemouth bass angler sticks the steel into a hybrid. Even though many use 20 pound test, a loud SNAP of the line is generally followed by some fancy cussin' and fussin'. Friends, that was no bucketmouth, 'twas a Rocket!

Loads of shad present wonderful growing opportunities to the sunshine bass here and the best times to catch them are during winter to and through spring. The lake gets 28 hybrid bass per acre annually, a very large number indeed.

I picked out a few other waters which the state told me are stocked to give you several more ideas.

Try Ocean Pond in Baker County where 20,000 palmetto/sunshine bass were stocked in recent years. The Medard Reservoir in Hillsborough County got over 80,000 in the 2003-2004 season.

The Caloosahatchee River in Hendry County got more than 50,000 in a recent year. And five lakes in Lake County (Eustis, BeauClaire, Carlton, Dora and Harris), received nearly 500,000 small fish between them in a four year span.

Last but not least, over at Santa Rosa County, more than 25,000 palmetto bass were stocked one year at the waters called FWC-BWFRC.

## ☑ GEORGIA — YES

According to Bill Baab, well-known outdoors writer with *The Augusta, Georgia Chronicle*, his state started stocking hybrid bass in 1977. South Carolina began stocking Clarks Hill Lake, which touches both states, in 1967 and Georgia began to add fish into it 10 years later.

The state rears hybrid bass at its Richmond Hill hatchery. Together, they annually stock approximately 700,000 fry (10 hybrid fry per acre) into the lake each spring. The lake is also called Strom Thurmond Lake and is an Army Corp. of Engineers facility, 30 miles north of Augusta. It is on the Savannah River.

Baab, like me, feels that hybrid bass are the absolute ultimate to catch and he rarely fishes for anything else. Clarks Hill Lake is his favorite stomping area and he can often be seen on it, with his wife, Bea and pet Yorkie on board his 16 foot deep-vee Larson.

If you would like to book a charter on the lake for hybrid bass, one guy you might want to contact would be Dan LaDow, who trades as Ace Striper Guide. His freebie number is 1-888-838-6305. The lake is the biggest in the state so a guide sure could help.

The lake houses both true strain and hybrid stripers in it and they feed aggressively on the large schools of blueback herring and threadfin shad that swim in its waters. Often seen, but never to be tired of, is the sight of a sky filled with sea gulls and terns diving into areas to gobble up the baitfish driven to the surface by feeding fish.

*Two big hybrids filled the cooler for Ted Boileau
out of Martinez, Georgia.*

Perhaps the most commonly used method at Clarks Hill is to rig with a live blueback herring, available at local bait stores, but Bill prefers to throw artificials. He generally chucks Zoom Super Flukes, Gotcha Shad, along with Berry's Flex-It or CC Spoons into the surface action. Casting blind also brings strikes and when you cannot see feeding fish, this can bring an even better charge to your battery when a sudden, out of nowhere, slam occurs.

Springtime is trolling time when fish are hiding and his lure of choice is a Gotcha Shad on a ⅜ ounce lead head jig.

Lots of people who work for the state provided assistance. Ed Bettross was the biologist with Georgia's DNR who referred Bill to me. And Dan Forster, Director of the state's Wildlife Resources Division gave me a wealth of data, as well as referring Senior Fisheries Biologist Bettross to me. And back in 2002, I got assistance too from Chris Martin, Aquatic Education Coordinator.

Director Forster said that 20 plus reservoirs and lakes are stocked yearly with these aggressive, hard-fighting fish. He said that their goal is to stock 1 to 1½ inch fish each spring, usually mid-April to early May.

This timing coincides with the shad and herring spawn which provides lots of food for the tiny hybrid to feed on. And feed they do, with the baby fish reaching as much as a foot in length by their first autumn. The herring and shad spawns annually produce enormous quantities of youngsters to also help feed the wide variety of other predators found in the waters of Georgia.

Mr. Forster told me that Georgia's state record hybrid bass was the whopping 25½ pound beast taken by David Hobby at Lake Chatuge in May of 1995.

Other than waters that border with South Carolina, which have a 10 fish limit, Georgia allows its anglers to harvest 15 fish daily and there are no size limits. This doesn't mean though that all caught should be taken home.

Throwing weighted cast nets seems to be the style of choice used by serious hybrid bass anglers in Georgia. Catching live bait and keeping them in a big live-well, with chemical additives, is a must if you want to hit your fish on live bait.

Although many tackle stores do carry live bait, there is nothing that beats those that are netted in the wild. (Ever hear of "wild shiners," ala Lake Okeechobee fame in Florida for huge bucket-mouth bass?)

We discussed Seminole Lake when we talked about Florida, because the lake is in both states. The biggest hybrid caught there was a 16.5 pounder back in 1975 and Georgia said that it has lots of hydrilla on its shallow waters which total 37,500 acres.

Some other big lakes that house loads of Rockets are Oconee, a 19,050 acre, heavily developed spot that is on the Oconee River in the piedmont, which gets 20 youngsters stocked annually. And one of the best known lakes in the entire state is Hartwell, second biggest at 56,000 acres and on the Savannah River in the northeast part of Georgia.

10 small fish per acre go into Walter F. George and West Point Lakes yearly. Both are on the Chattahoochee River. George (45,180 acres) is in southwest Georgia and West Point (25,900 acres) is between Columbus and Atlanta.

An article in the *Georgia Outdoor News* told of the action

involving West Point fish that swim up the Chattahoochee at the Franklin Shoals area each spring. They attempt to spawn and since hybrid bass aren't capable of doing that in Georgia, their second best choice, I guess, is to eat!

Fly fishermen hit the river each winter in search of the hybrids, and often do well. But be warned that if you are like me and always seem to find the most slippery green rocks, it may be a good idea to not try to walk on water. I feel that I have invented what I call the "Green Rock Flop" but I know that more guys than me have gone backwards down a river.

But if you are a pro, and have a fly reel loaded with lots of backing, and have the guts to try, prepare for the wildest fight of your life on a river. Yes, a 50 pound chinook is a beast indeed, but pound for pound, I still prefer hybrid bass.

Back to the spring action. Brad Gill was the writer who reported that Guide Paul Parsons (1-800-224-8892) produces goodly numbers of hybrids for customers while trolling curly tails and Sassy Shads in front of the dam. But up into the river often gives even better action early in spring.

Try anchoring up in the first bend of the river, just below the Franklin Bridge — this works quite well. Parsons throws a castnet early each morning to catch a mess of live shad as bait. Live or cut, both styles work. And it is illegal to use blueback herring as bait in West Point, so don't even think about that.

Frozen shad and chicken liver, discussed in the Florida section, both produce action while on anchor. I like to feed over little bits of cut bait to use as chum but if the current is strong, a frozen chum log placed into one of those cylindrical containers and dropped to the bottom will gather feeding fish to your slick. Of course a hooked hybrid may want to play ring around the pot so you may have to abort this style if your fish get you snagged into the pot line too often.

Summertime hybrid lovers often head to Hartwell Lake which also holds lots of big true-strain striped bass. Some people like to drift but I still prefer to double-anchor my boat and fish straight down.

An article in *The Citizen* said that fishing in 25-40 feet of water with live bream or shad will produce action. You can also buy blueback herring at local tackle stores.

Since you could get inhaled by a monster true-strain, you may want to go with heavier line than my usually preferred six or eight pound mono. 15-20 may be better and make sure you test your knots to and from your barrel swivel and hook. A "curly cue" (a knot that opens) could really mess up your whole day, especially if you have a witness who might blackmail you to avoid telling other friends about it.

# HAWAII — NO

Hawaii told me that when they introduced largemouth and smallmouth bass into the state, the native freshwater fauna suffered a negative impact, even though residents enjoyed catching them. And there really aren't more than a few lakes that can be found in the state that don't head out into moving water which can then drop into the ocean. But, having been there, I know that there are at least a few lakes that the fish (and residents plus tourists) might be happy in but, for now, the word remains negative.

# IDAHO — NO

When I heard from Resident Fishery Coordinator Fred Partridge several years ago, he was quite familiar with the white/striped bass cross. He told me that the state of Idaho doesn't have a sufficient volume of forage in its lakes to support another bait gobbler like hybrid bass.

Between the walleyes plus large and smallmouth bass present, and the limited volume of bait fish, there just didn't seem to be room for my favorite fish. Hopefully though, this could change.

# ILLINOIS — YES

Back in 2002, Mike Conlin, who was Chief of the Illinois Division of Fisheries, reported that his state does indeed stock hybrid bass, as well as striped bass. Illinois has already produced at least one hybrid in excess of 20 pounds, even though it is a bit to

ILLINOIS

*Illinois state record hybrid which was caught 6/23/86 by Dennis Carroll. This fish weighed 15 lbs. 4.8 oz.*

the north of the states that may be better known to hold hybrids.

He calls them a SUPER sport fish, and if you have had one break your line, you know he is right. Illinois stocks the fish into larger impoundments which hold adequate supplies of gizzard shad forage. He further said that the fish do well in power plant cooling lakes which have warm water discharges and flow.

My guess is that this means that, even in cold times, you can catch some near the outfalls which produce a comfortable volume of warmer water. Where legal to do, anchor close to the outfall and get ready to be slammed. This can also be done at venues that offer shoreline access to any such discharges.

Joe Ferencak, Impoundment Program Manager, sent me still more useful material late in 2004.

Some of the lakes that have been stocked with hybrid bass in the state include:

## LaSalle Lake

LaSalle Lake is a 2,058 acre cooling lake in LaSalle County, up in the northwest section of the state. It was opened in 1987 for public fishing and hybrid stockings began three years later.

A strong gizzard and threadfin shad population is present, giving the fish plenty of food to grow quickly on. Back in 1996, a creel survey showed that only channel catfish and white bass were caught in larger numbers by local anglers. Be careful to avoid windy days because when it cranks up, you had better already be back at the barn.

## Lake George

Lake George, and no, not the huge one in upstate New York, is a modest-sized impoundment in Rock Island County that gets lots of fishing pressure in its 167 acres. Large numbers of fish have been stocked into the lake since hybrid bass began being added in 1997.

Before '97, gizzard shad were plopped into the lake by an unknown party and their population exploded, but when hybrids went in, a bit of a reduction occurred, as only a mess of hybrid can cause.

## Heidecke Lake

Heidecke Lake is in the northeast area of the state, situated near Morris, Grundy County, and it houses both pure and hybrid stripers. The lake was the home of record true and hybrid stripers for quite a while. Catches of 10 plus pounders are still commonly made.

The state takes sample nettings often and in a 2000 netting, they found hybrids that went from year-olds to 10 pound Rockets, with the average being $19\frac{1}{2}$ inches, weighing over 3 pounds.

The nearly 2000 acre lake also has a goodly number of white bass in it, meaning that in a good day, an angler can catch a "Grand Slam" of sorts here, True stripers, white bass, and their sterile off-spring, hybrid bass, my favorite, of course. I hear tell that it may even have some yellow bass in it.

Watch the wind here too, and be sure to obey the regulation that requires you to have a well-working gasoline engine (for your own safety as well as to comply with the law). The lake opens at 6:00 a.m. and closes at sunset, and a bait and tackle plus boat rental operation is present.

### Clinton Lake

Clinton Lake is in the center of the state. There are separate regulations that prevail here, including open and closed seasons so be sure you are in compliance. No-wake, electric motor only areas exist also.

This is a very large lake at 4,895 acres and was among the first in the state to get hybrid bass way back in 1978. Flash floods put a big dent in the fishery in the 90's but large stockings went in afterwards, cranking the population back up, big time.

For example, 28,000 two inchers went in during 1999. True strain and white bass are also here, giving you yet another chance at a "Grand Slam."

A few other central Illinois lakes that house hybrids are Pittsfield and Jacksonville.

### Otter Lake

Otter Lake is in the southwest portion of the state and it too is a fine venue to seek your hybrid bass in. Fish in excess of 12 pounds have been brought to the net in Otter.

### Baldwin Lake

Baldwin Lake can be found in District 17, but it seems to be a bit too warm in the summer to assist hybrid bass in growing to larger size. However, with 19,000 babies added yearly, there sure is nothing wrong with catching a five-pound Rocket, is there?

The state has taken nettings from the tip of the cross dike in mid-autumn, and samplings have shown an average weight of 3.32 pounds.

### Crab Orchard Lake

Crab Orchard Lake is big for Illinois at 7,000 acres (2½ times bigger than anything we have in New Jersey, for example), and it too has some special closed season regulations. Situated in Williamstown County, a miles south of Carterville, the lake has gotten some rather large stockings of hybrid bass into it.

Tournaments are held on the lake (after holders first get preregistered) and when the boys with the big sparkle plenty boats are on the water, you had better watch out, 'cause they go fast!

### Shabbona

Another lake that has hybrid bass in it is Shabbona in northwest Illinois. Little at 319 acres, lit has walleye, muskellunge, as well as hybrid bass so give it a shot.

A few more places are Lake of Egypt and Washington County Lake ("Wascho").

### Pool 14 of the Mississippi River

Pool 14 of the Mississippi River has had hybrid stocked into it by a unique threesome, Exelon (formerly Commonwealth Edison), Southern Illinois University, and the state (IDNR"), combined to bring yearling babies into the river.

River-reared hybrid bass may test your drag even more than lake fish because they grow stronger while fighting current. So try for a trophy at Pool 14, but make sure your drag runs smooth or prepare to hear that awful sound, SNAP!

Doggone near each lake that has hybrid bass in it has its own bag limit as well as other rules so, please, get a compendium and read up before heading out. Of course if you practice catch and release, rules will be far easier to deal with, right?

# ☑ INDIANA — YES

19 pounds, three ounces! That was the weight of the heaviest hybrid bass ever caught in Indiana when it came out of the Tippecanoe River back in 2002 by Sam Tracy. And pardon the pun (one that no doubt was used often that year), Sam sure had to be careful because otherwise, he might have (sorry) tipped his canoe over. My guess is that he was in a far bigger boat than a canoe though.

And who knows, by the time you read this book, a "20" may have beaten his fish at that. For those who don't fish for carp, by the way, a "20" signifies a fish that weighs at least twenty pounds.

Brian Schoenung, South Region Fisheries Supervisor in Indiana, loves to fish for hybrid bass himself. In fact, he took the photo you will see on the books' cover of co-worker, Dave Kittaka, who is a

*Photo by Brian Schoenung*

*Sam Tracy holding his state record 19.3 lb. hybrid,*
*caught at the Tippecanoe River.*

district biologist with the state. Dave's 11 pounder was caught while trolling a stick bait and was promptly released after Brian snapped the photo.

Far and away the most popular lake for hybrid bass in Indiana is Lake Monroe, which is also the largest lake that gets the fish (5 per acre) at 10,750 acres. Brian said that spring time is very good, as well as during the autumn, especially near the dam. He likes to use surface lures and shallow crank baits. Come summer, main lake points near the creek channel are best and the best methods involve anglers who throw diving crank baits as well as live bait.

Indiana began stocking hybrid bass in the 80's, and those waters on the stocking list include, in addition to Monroe, the following:

| Body of water | Acres | # Stocked per acre |
|---|---|---|
| Lake Freeman | 1,547 | 10 |
| Nyona Lake | 104 | 10 |
| Shadyside Park Pond * | 63 | 16 |
| Cedar Lake | 781 | 10 |
| Lake Shafer | 1,291 | 10 |
| Clare Lake* | 42 | 10 |

*Shadyside Park Pond and Clare Lake are usually stocked in even years only.*

Here are directions to some of the above bodies of water that hold hybrid bass in Indiana, courtesy of Chicago Fishing Links.com's site:

In LaGrange County, Cedar Lake is four miles north-east of Howe. Take CR600N to CR325 and then north for ¼ of a mile.

Lake Freeman is in White County. Take SR24 to Monticello and head east of St. Mary's Ave.

The Tippecanoe River holds lots of hybrid bass (The record was taken there) and one section that produces hybrids can be found in White County, north of Monticello. Take Francis Street to the Norway Dam Public Fishing Area.

And in Fulton County, to get to Nyona Lake, head one mile north of Fulton on SR25 and then five miles east on CR650S.

The state usually stocks its hybrid fingerlings each June, but production of youngsters was down in 2004 so only Lake Monroe was stocked that year.

# 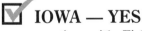 IOWA — YES

I had a pleasant conversation with Fisheries Chief Marion Conover a few years ago and he agreed that, yes, "They ARE Rockets!" when I told him what I call them. He said that the Des Moines River System was the best area in Iowa for hybrid bass, between Saylorville and Red Rock Lakes. The fish have been in such waters since the early 80's.

Dick McWilliams handles most of the hybrid stockings in his

IOWA

*"Fish Iowa" is what the cap on Mark Boucher's head says.*
*Iowa co-worker Chris Larson took the shot during one of their*
*samplings at Lake Manawa.*

area of the state. Besides the above waters, Dick said that others
also have sizeable populations of hybrid.

Among them are Coralville Reservoir, over in the eastern
section of Iowa, and over to the west, Lake Manawa. Further, that
in order to reduce prey fish population, Big Creek Lake received

loads of hybrid bass during the period 1996 to 2002. In fact, upwards of 350,000 small fry went in.

Big Creek Lake covers 883 acres and goes as deep as 52 feet. You can use any size outboard engine but the lake is a "no-wake" one so crank it down, please. The lake is found two miles north of Polk City on Highway 415. There are five boat ramps on this relatively small lake, as well as a number of jetties that you can fish from.

Big Creek Lake is adjacent to Saylorville Reservoir which received hybrid fry since 1981 on just about an annual basis. For the years 2003 and 2004 though, larger fingerlings went into the reservoir.

Since being established at Saylorville, quite a few fish have headed out and into the Des Moines River system. They have been taken upstream near Fort Dodge and as far downstream as Ottumwa. www.iowadnr.com said that hybrid bass should be found all the way to the Mississippi River.

As of 2004, the record was taken in the Des Moines River below Saylorville in 1997 and it weighed an ounce under 19 pounds, measuring 33¼ inches overall. Go back to 1985 and it was held with another Des Moines River hybrid at only 8 plus pounds. That one was landed below Red Rock Reservoir.

Being a bit to the north of the country, Iowa presents its best fishing time during late summer, as we have in New Jersey. Mr. McWilliams said that the fish feed at most any time of the day at all, as he said, "when they're on," so it will behoove anglers in Iowa to spend lots of time on the pond in order to catch them when feeding time is present.

(Check out what I call "Magic Hour" as well as "Solunar Time" in the start of the book to get a few ideas on several specific good times to give it a go.) He added that once you locate white bass on your lake, hybrid bass tend to hang below them so if you catch a white or two, fish deeper and you should locate hybrid bass right there.

KANSAS

## ☑ KANSAS — YES

Kansas was the very first state to get back to me with answers when I outreached to all 50 states for help in 2004 regarding my hybrid book so let me put into print now this very simple THANK YOU to Kansas for their prompt and thorough response.

Back in 2002, Doug Nygren, Fisheries Section Chief was the person who gave me material. In 2004, it was Kyle Austin, Fisheries Management Coordinator at the Pratt Operations Office.

Kyle said that his state has been stocking hybrid bass (They call them Palmetto, or Wiper) since the early 80's. The heaviest wiper taken out of Kansas waters was the 22 pound heavyweight nailed by Kevin Carson of Osage City, Kansas. Kevin was using sodworms at Pomona Reservoir on 6/28/93 when he brought the fish in.

The state can provide you with a very handy brochure which reports on a variety of subjects regarding the fish that are in her waters. You can find out such things as how many largemouth bass are in Logan City Lake and how big are the crappie (black and white) taken from Cedar Bluff Reservoir in state samplings, as well as a bazillion other very interesting things.

To get a copy, write to Fisheries & Wildlife Division, Kansas Department of Wildlife and Parks, 512 SE 25th Avenue, Pratt, Kansas 67124 and request the "Kansas Fishing Forecast." It comes out annually, near the end of January.

The brochure offers statistics on subjects like the largest fish of each species that they have found in their samplings (not the biggest fish in the lakes, just the weight of the heaviest they got in their nettings). They list the size of each water, as well as their own rating of the lakes for each kind of fish, by "density," "lunker' and "preferred."

Density is defined as the number of fish that were quality size in the state's samplings. Preferred tells which lakes have above average fish. And, simple enough, lunker is how many of the larger Palmetto bass were found in the reservoir/lake.

If you don't see a listing of big critters in your favorite venue, that doesn't mean that they aren't there. It just means that the

*Bruce Condello with his 32¼ inch striped bass hybrid at Cedar Bluff Reservoir near Wakeeney, Kansas.*

beasts were hiding when the netting was going on!

For example, we pointed out that the state record 22 pounder came out of Pomona Reservoir but the heaviest found when the netting was done only hit 6.60 pounds. And over at Cedar Bluff Reservoir, 10.08 was the heavyweight in the netting. But hybrid lover Bruce Condello has caught several that were far heavier.

The 2004 Forecast brochure listed 11 reservoirs and 26 lakes that were netted. And that only includes the waters that Kansas sampled. Quite a few more waters also get Palmetto's and weren't netted.

Here are the waters that were found to have the largest number of quality fish in 2004. First listed are the reservoirs and then the smaller lakes. Starting by name, and then by acreage, and lastly, by number of good fish (a foot long or better) netted:

| Reservoir | Size of water (acres) | Density |
|---|---|---|
| Marion | 6,160 | 40.67 |
| Webster | 3,500 | 38.51 |
| Sebelius | 1,500 | 35.30 |
| Cedar Bluff | 6,500 | 20.00 |
| Kirwin | 4,000 | 19.65 |
| Cheney | 9,550 | 15.00 |

| Lake | Size of water | Density |
|---|---|---|
| Wellington City Lake | 700 | 65 |
| Sabetha-Pony Creek Lake | 171 | 51 |
| Marion Co. Lake | 153 | 31 |
| Douglas Co.-Lonestar Lake | 195 | 26.50 |
| Plainville Lake | 100 | 16.08 |

Not even shown in the above list are wonderful other reservoirs like the 16,020 acre Milford impoundment which certainly holds loads of big hybrid bass. Ditto Pomona, a 4,000 acre reservoir, which produced the record fish in 1993.

As an example of how serious Kansas is about their hybrid bass stocking program, the 2004 stocking list showed that the Milford Fish Hatchery alone produced nearly NINE MILLION little critters that year. Fry are raised there and grown out in that hatchery as well as at the Pratt and Farlington Hatcheries.

If you check out your map of the original 48 states you will see that Kansas sits right smack dab in the middle of the country. Therefore, if you want to give my favorite fish a try, start at Kansas and work your way around in a circle outward. Make sure you have lots of time to fish each state and, obviously, be properly licensed and have full knowledge of all the rules and regulations.

A camper with trailered boat behind might be the best way to go. That circle would include Colorado, Nebraska, Missouri, and

Oklahoma. And, what the heck, if you have a 100 days to spare, outreach even further. For sure, if you catch hybrid bass in any volume at all, you too will be as badly hooked as we lunatic Rocket lovers have become.

I read an article in the Great Plains Game & Fish web site which reported on what their writer, Tim Lilley, felt were the top hybrid waters in the state and, of course, you will see that most are listed already in the stuff the state gave me. They include these reservoirs-La Cygne, Pomona and Milford in the east, and out west, Webster, Cedar Bluff, Kirwin and Sebelius. Now add in Milford Lake, mid-state, shown above in the lake list.

Some folks around the county feel that largemouth bass fishing is hurt by the introduction of hybrid bass as competitors for food. But other than the very smallest of impoundments, that really isn't the case. Most hybrid activity takes place far away from the shoreline where the bucketmouth brigade is working.

Mr. Lilley's article went on to point out that May is the best time of the year in Kansas for wipers. He favors jigs, spinner baits or a lipless crankbait. Trolling produces lots of action for him as well as casting.

You will read throughout the book that I personally favor live bait fishing, but a mixture of two styles may be your best bet if you have the skill to manage it. You will need a day with modest wind and a good quality electric motor.

Instead of dragging plugs, try a live bait, via trolling. Use a one ounce egg sinker, stop it with a dark barrel swivel, and attach a three foot leader. Fasten a size 6 model 3906 Mustad to the line and bait the hook with your live critter of choice. Either hook it through the mouth and out an eye hole, or stick the hook through each eye socket. If you have a child with you, try to do this without them watching, or lie a bit and say that the baitfish like to have you help them learn how to swim this way.

If you hook a hybrid while trolling, I sure hope your drag was open, or else you will be quickly broken off, or worse ... your rod will jump out of the boat as quick as you can blink your eyes! Enjoy Rockets, we who have caught them sure do!

# Introduction to Midword

Honestly, I never had a "Midword" in any of my thirteen prior books, and I don't even know if it is a legitimate word, but when I found Bruce Condello, I knew that I had to have some material from him and therefore, came up with the term, "Midword" to give him space to talk to you about our favorite fish in this book.

Bruce practices dentistry in Lincoln, Nebraska, and catches lots of his hybrid bass right from the beach at Cedar Bluff Reservoir in Kansas. Briefly, taking just a very little out of the list of excellent credits he gave me, Bruce is a licensed aquaculturist who raises wipers for sportfishing interests in Nebraska. He holds ten National Fresh Water Fishing Hall of Fame line class world records for catching and releasing a variety of fish, including five hybrid bass, in 2, 4 and 6 pound test.

Bruce's writings have been featured in a variety of publications such as the Lincoln Journal-Star (Nebraska), and In-Fisherman magazine. Check him out at www.wipercentral.net.

Photo from Bruce Condello

# Midword

*By Bruce Condello*

*Bruce, a dentist by profession, having his 31 inch hybrid say "Ahh" before returning it into a lake near Denton, Nebraska.*

"It seems we live in a world that every recreational endeavor requires higher and higher levels of sophistication. Fishing is no different. Boats are bigger, electronics are fancier and fishing motors are more powerful than ever. We're inundated with images of fishermen who participate in tournaments with thirty-thousand dollar rigs who peer deeply into color LCD screens hoping to pinpoint a single fish who might want to strike at their twenty-five dollar crankbait. We're led to believe that fishing has become a sport for the rich and privileged.

Fortunately, for those of us who are shore bound there exists a fish that grows to mammoth proportions, but can be reached with the toss of a quarter-ounce bucktail jig. The striped bass hybrid is a hockey player amongst ballerinas. Better make sure your equipment is in perfect working condition, because if it's not, the hybrid will disassemble the reel right in your hands.

Every spring striped bass hybrids follow the urges of reproduction that take them far into the shallows. Highly oxygenated down wind points invite hybrids right into range for skinny water anglers. It's not unusual for the wading angler to watch a two-foot long hybrid create a manhole cover sized boil right at the rod tip as it swipes at a bucktail jig or swimbait.

If you don't believe it then you're just going to have to try it for yourself. Ask your state fishery biologist about locating a lake with a good population of hybrid. Gather information about springtime water temperatures and target a time of year with temperatures in the mid-50's to mid-60's. Find a downwind point that gives you access to a little deeper water and get ready to step foot into the hybrid's realm. Ideal tackle would include 6-8 pound test monofilament and a bright pink or chartreuse bucktail with a stout, sharp hook.

Remember, not many fish have the potential to reach such stupendous sizes as the striped bass hybrid. Many states with hybrid programs list state records at over fifteen pounds and some as high as twenty-five! These fish, especially the bigger ones, should be treated with the reverence and respect they deserve. Releasing striped bass hybrids is easy to do in waders and will leave room on your stringer for other fish that you'll likely be catching such as white bass and white perch. Don't bypass the opportunity to give a captured hybrid the chance to embarrass another fisherman with a mind-bending run. You won't regret it."

# ☑ KENTUCKY — YES

We all know about "Kentucky Bass," a strain of largemouth that is extremely popular and for good reason, but the fine state of Kentucky also holds many thousands of hybrid bass. So let's talk about them without saying much more about the big-mouth variety for now.

When I wrote that article for a magazine about these critters in 2002, Ted Crowell was the man who responded from Kentucky. He said that he was glad that I finally discovered this fish (I had caught my first in 1993 so it wasn't as if I had never seen one before 2002, but I didn't tell him that then). He also said that he doubted that I was going to have success in renaming it. But, hey, if I hook just some of you in each state and you tell friends that this is indeed a critter quite similar to a ROCKET, then hey, I can wait!

Ted said that the state stocked 702,000 hybrid stripers into nine waters in 2002 and that they started their program more than 20 years ago. Their state record Rocket weighed 20½ pounds, and was caught by Mark Wilson at Barren River tailwater on 4/27/91. Nice!

This last time around, my response came from Jim Axon of the Kentucky Dept. of Fish and Wildlife Resources. Here are some of the very interesting details Jim gave me.

## Barren River Lake

Barren River Lake was first stocked in 1979, making it among the first waters in Kentucky to get them. The 60 plus foot deep lake is usually stocked with 200,000 1½-inch long babies. Its tailwaters also hold lots of hybrid bass. Colonel Jesse Duncan, another of the folks I have stumbled upon who idolize hybrid bass, told me that the lake has a dissolved oxygen problem but still has good water 20 feet down in the deep summer.

## Rough River Lake

Rough River Lake and tailwater also have lots of youngsters stocked yearly. The program began there in 1995 and the stocking tally is 102,000 1½ inchers yearly.

## Taylorsville Lake

Taylorsville Lake began receiving hybrid in 1989 and it gets 60,000 1½-inch fish.

*Colonel Jesse Duncan showing off his 9.4 lb. Kentucky fly rod class record. Caught at Barren River Lake.*

### Herrrington Lake

Herrrington Lake also had its hybrid bass start-up program begin in 1979 and it currently gets 50,000 fish.

### Fishtrap Lake

Fishtrap Lake has received hybrid since 1990 and the current number is 23,000. Its tailwater is a good place to try for these speedsters.

### The Ohio River

The Ohio River got hybrid bass starting in 1995 and it currently received its youngsters from adjoining states Ohio and West Virginia along the river.

Other waters that hold hybrid bass include, but are not limited to: Grayson Lake and its tailwater, the lower Green River, the Tennessee River below Lake Barkley, and the Cumberland River below Kentucky Lake. As noted earlier, if you can best a hybrid that was reared fighting the current of a river, friend, you have had the very best you can get.

There are several articles I found in the Kentucky Game & Fish web site that I turned to for further assistance, both having been written by Norm Minch.

One piece said that Lake Cumberland is a place that you can target true-strain striped bass as well as hybrids. The large lake (50,000 plus acres) coughed up a striper that doggone near hit 60 pounds back in the 80's. Of course it is my opinion that if you hooked a 20 plus hybrid it could pull a 40 plus true-strain backwards, but a near-60? I dunno.

Mr. Minch also said that good catches of hybrid bass have been made in Herrington Lake, in the center of the state, and at Taylorsville Lake, both noted earlier.

Kentucky, like several other states that contain hybrid bass, has different bag and even size limits so please be absolutely certain you are up on the rules and regulations of the lake/river that you are fishing. The state has some water that contains true-strain but it also holds white bass in quite a few places so, once again, know the rules.

Back in the start of the book we talked about how and where to catch these beasts in general, so rather than repeating it all again, I suggest you head back to the "Where and how" part. For sure, surface plugs are wonderful and when you get slammed and the critter throws the plastic offering skyward, not getting hooked, it is time to DUCK! Jigs as well as live bait all produce, but again, head back to the where and how, okay?

## ☑ LOUISIANA — YES

He may be a bit biased, but Ronnie Christ told me that Lake Clairborne is the best hybrid bass lake in all of Louisiana. Of course he should know though, because he works for the state out of District 1, near where the big lake is.

Clairborne is also the largest lake in the state with hybrids at just about 6,300 acres. It goes down to 50 feet deep in spots and has the usual dissolved oxygen situation we have discussed so

*Concordia - Louisiana fisheries biologists Jackie Wiseman (on truck) and Dave Hickman, finishing off a stocking of fingerlings at Lake Concordia.*

often in the book. Simply though, when your bait dies 25 feet down, plop the next one down five feet less, and if it croaks there, put bait #3 at 15 feet and chances are good to excellent that you will be in the hot strike zone.

Clairborne anglers often see that wonderful sight of hybrid bass busting bait on top here. The lake is situated near the town of Homer. (By the way, I generally refer to a "town" unless I am talking about a big city. So if I insult your "borough," "village," "hamlet," "parish," etc., by calling it a "town," then, please excuse me.)

District 4 has three nice lakes that hold hybrid bass. Each gets approximately 10 1½-inch fingerlings yearly, based on available stock. The lakes are:

Bruin, near the town of St. Joseph, at 2,342 acres and with a depth of 25 feet or so.

Concordia, which is partially in the town of Ferriday. Concordia is smaller at 1,050 acres and the main lake is only a dozen feet deep or so. When it was first stocked in 1995, it was jump started with the placement of 100,000 small critters. It connects to Little Blue Hole which goes to 30-40 feet, and to Big Blue Hole which is as deep as 50 feet near the old broken levee.

Hybrid bass were raised at the Toledo Bend Hatchery but Ronnie Christ told me that the Booker Fowler Hatchery would take over the program in 2005.

Gary Tilyou, Assistant administrator for the State's Inland Fisheries Division first responded to me in 2002 with some wonderful help and came back again with lots more three years later.

Between 1999 and 2002, the Department stocked over 1,800,000 true-strain striper fingerlings into Louisiana waters! So this state likes both critters. Those hybrids that they started stocking in 2004 were what are called "Reciprocal Cross," being produced from male striped bass and female white bass.

The state began stocking hybrid bass in the 70's and largemouth bass and crappie anglers were none too happy to see their fish at the dining table in competition with hybrid bass. But Gary said that they sure did create a group of hybrid fishermen that greatly enjoyed the new fishery. And by now, peaceful co-existence seems to be in place.

Another lake that holds hybrid bass, according to www.fishinglouisiana.com, is Caddo Lake, at the Louisiana-Texas border near Caddo Parish in La. This puddle is 25,400 acres in size and you will need to comply with regulations that may differ because of it being found in two states, so let the angler beware.

That same site reported that D'Arbonne Lake, between Union and Lincoln, a mostly open water lake, had both hybrid and true-strain stripers in it. And when you are open water, try to fish in the deepest sections, off of any point of land you can find.

Find the depth that holds bait alive in summer and get down there while sitting on double-anchors. Open your drag, grab a cool drink, and rest, because the next sound you may hear could be screaming drag, oh, yeah!

## MAINE — NO

Here's the first of five states in a row that don't stock hybrid bass. Perhaps Maine, being so far north, is one of the few that really cannot accommodate a hybrid fishery because they need warmer water than present in most of the state. (But check out the few that are at least as far north that have them in!)

But don't worry about folks who live in Maine. The state stocks about 1,200,000 trout and salmon into her waters annually. And they have excellent naturally wild fisheries for both small and largemouth bass.

## MARYLAND — NO

Maryland made the decision some time ago to not introduce hatchery-raised fish into her waters, feeling that this is not a substitute for natural capacity. (Hopefully, that wasn't a permanent decision, and maybe you can write to your Department of Natural Resources to ask them to change their minds).

They did point out that they have freshwater striped bass opportunities found in Liberty, Piney Run, Triadelphia, Conowingo, and Rocky Gorge Reservoirs. And, of course, good fishing is available along their coast.

## MASSACHUSETTS — NO

Sorry, I guess, for now, folks up thattaway will have be satisfied that their baseball team finally beat the Yankees, and that their football team usually beats everyone else. Sure, some very fine lakes are popular and the ocean action is often superb. But even though the climate is colder than preferred by hybrid bass at some times of the year, I bet that a few lakes could easily handle a Rocket fishery. One day, maybe, I hope.

## MICHIGAN — NO

At times, a hybrid bass escapee from elsewhere might get into Lake Erie and get caught but the state doesn't intentionally put them into any of her waters. The state considered putting true-strain striped bass in back in the 80's and rejected that idea, but they do have lots of lakes that have considerable populations of white bass.

# ⊘ MINNESOTA — NO

Yes, it's kind of chilly up Minnesota way, and that may be the main reason for the state not putting hybrid bass into any of its waters. Hybrids just cannot thrive in water that is solid on top for an extended period of time. So the good people of Minnesota will have to "settle" with the excellent stocking program their state has for walleye, as well as muskellunge and trout.

Allen Stevens, Lake and stream program consultant with the state's DNR told me that more than 900 hundred lakes are stocked with walleye either as fry or fingerling. And the state also has naturally producing largemouth and smallmouth bass. Mr. Stevens added that hybrid bass fry were stocked in Lake Pepin, a border state shared with Wisconsin way back in the late 70's, but they were never seen again.

# ☑ MISSISSIPPI — YES

The state with the most double-letters began stocking pure striped bass back in 1968 into Ross Barnett Reservoir. Its hybrid program was initiated in 1977 when Grenada Lake got 140,000 1½ inchers, and the program continues to please residents.

One of the super additional benefits that Mississippi gets as a result of its stocking pure striped bass into Ross Barnett is that they recover adult fish at the spillway and they are collected for brood stock by the Turcotte Hatchery. And if that isn't a unique example of "Recycling," tell me what is.

Several people from the state provided assistance to me about their program. First, in 2002, and again in 2005, was Chief Ron Garavelli. Fisheries Biologist Tom Holman, from whom Ron suggested I get more information, was extremely helpful.

Among the largest stockings of hybrid fingerlings into Mississippi in '02 went into Ross Barnett, with 300,000 yearly (!), and Eagle Lake at 30,000. Other state lakes include Lake Charlie Capps in Bolivar County, and Bogue Homa Lake in Laurel.

*Mississippi Technician, Jonathan Lucas (foreground) and Curtis Summerlin, Hatchery Manager, "milking" a striper parent to get the mixing process underway.*

Now add in a few more. Okatibbee Reservoir near Meridian and Oktibbeha County Lake also get young hybrid bass.

Last but not least is the river that bears the state's name. The Mississippi is not really stocked by the state but as Tom Holman said, "I guess just about every other state in the drainage does." He added that when the water's right, the wing dikes and jetties above Vicksburg can be awesome. But he also warned that it could also be dangerous so by all means, be very careful here.

The jury is out regarding whether hybrid bass have been known to actually reproduce, even though they were initially reared to be sterile. However, a bunch of adult hybrid in the river make a spawning (or maybe a pseudo spawning) run up the Yazoo River Basin. The can be found in large number each spring at Army Corp. of Engineers dams like Sardis, Grenada and Enid. In such waters, you had better have big reels with lots of good line or prepare to get spooled by these bolts of lightning.

Spring stockings involve 1-2-inch fingerlings. Some states stock bigger ones and many usually put fry in. Because of their small size, candy corn to bigger predators, mortality is high with 70% or more not making it to the second year. But they grown quickly, reaching a foot by the end of the first year. And at year two, they are already 15-17 inchers or better, and by their third year, many will get up to 7-9 pounds. They generally live to six years of age but, of course, some make it further. Because they have so long a feeding season, being in such a warm climate, they can get all the way up into the 20's in weight.

Here's some more tips from Mr. Holman. Spring action is often the best, especially around spillway dams when the fish try to do their spawning thing. Heavy jigs and slab spoons are Tom's lures of choice. If you can see fish chasing schooling shad on top, suspend a smaller jig below a popping cork and just bring it back to you with an erratic retrieve. A surface Zara Spook also is effective.

Come summer, fish are looking for cooler water so check out creek or river channels or fish close to a dam. Your fish finder is critical here because instead of fishing blind, finding a school of baitfish on your recorder can save you lots of down time.

When heavily concentrated, they appear as a large blob and in fact, you can get an artificially created incorrect depth reading. Here you are, in 25 feet, and all of a sudden, your machine shows you are in ten feet. Chances are that you have begun to pass over a huge pile of bait that is riding ten feet below you. Get ready, 'cause it's time to get serious. Quite often, you will see surface action also.

Tom suggests trying to troll for hybrid bass in Eagle Lake. May might be the best month for this style. It doesn't have many stumps for you to hang up on but as warned elsewhere, make sure your drag is kind of loose.

Sure, you can tighten it up and stick the rod in a fine rod holder. But all the holder will ensure for you is that you have a great chance at getting your rod broken into two pieces. Light line and tight drag mean broken line. Heavy line and tight drag and rod holder means you got a rod stump left because the rest of the deal got snapped off.

An article in the www.mississippigameandfish.com written by Robert H. Cleveland, suggests trolling about 10-15 yards offshore of the piers and boathouses from Muddy Bayou to the boat ramp on the east end. He then added that after reaching the ramp, continue to Garfield Landing. Watch your depth finder and stay on the deeper side. As is standard clear across the country, Mr. Cleveland pointed out that these fine fish can often be seen clobbering bait on top early or late in the day. It's times like this that makes an angler feel that it just doesn't get any better.

## ☑ MISSOURI — YES

In recent years, Missouri has stocked a good number of lakes and reservoirs with young hybrid bass. Many states go with babies that average an-inch and one half. Others try it with mere fry in far larger number because of limited survival rates. Still others stock fish that average four inches, like Bob Papson does in New Jersey.

Missouri has stocked its larger waters with young hybrid bass that go anywhere from an-inch to four inches. And they put four-inch youngsters into their smaller lakes. Each body of water receives its stockings every two to three years. And here's the list:

1- Lake of the Ozarks — this fine body of water is 55,000 acres big.

2 - Truman Lake, named, no doubt for the President who came from the Show-Me state, is a bit bigger than Lake of the Ozarks at 55,600 acres.

3 - Thomas Hill Lake is 4,950 acres.

4 - Blue Springs Lake is 720 acres.

5 - Cameron Reservoir #3 is only 96 acres in size but plenty big enough to support hybrids.

6 - Harmony Mission Lake, is another 96 acre lake with a nice population of Rockets.

7-11 - James A. Reed Memorial Wildlife Area is a five lake spot with ponds going anywhere from 14-42 acres in size.

The two largest impoundments get an average of 5.3 fish per

*Stocking, the easy way.*

acre at each stocking, making for one heck of a lot of little fish each time, nearly 30,000 babies. And the smaller lakes get even more fish per acre at every stocking.

Depending on available stock, they receive at least seven and as many as 25 fish per acre every two or three years. Missouri began stocking hybrid bass way back in the late 70's.

**#2, Truman** is in the west-central portion of the state and according to www.conservation.state.mo.us, also holds a nice population of white bass. The best action here takes place from June to September. They report both species being taken by vertically jigging spoons or jigs in the main lake areas wherever you can locate structure.

Your depth recorder can help you find changes in depth or submerged trees. Fishing the drop-offs adjacent to humps is a good style. Of course if you are machine-literate, and have a GPS or LORAN machine and know how to work it, than try to spend some time putting down the "numbers" of spots that produce for you. Chances are good to excellent that if you come back to them, fish will be on hand more often than not.

Gizzard shad are the food of choice on Truman so as we will tell you so often herein, "match the hatch," use lures that look like such forage, and you should score. Some guys swear by the use of Black Bombers by night and Yellow Bombers by day further to the north and for sure, neither looks like a shad. But they still work.

My stickbait of choice is still a Thin Fin. They come in a variety of colors, but purple, blue or black on top are the best. The belly will be shiny, like the baitfish they imitate. Most importantly, they are deep in the belly, just like the shad you are trying to copy.

As summer swings into place, baitfish may be seen trying to climb up invisible ladders into the sky as hybrid bass blast them out of the water. Now comes a test of your ability to concentrate. Prepare to throw surface plugs into the outer edges of the frenzy, but make sure you creep up slowly with electric power to avoid putting them down. At such times, even the most experienced anglers may get nuts and in a clumsy and too fast attempt at casting out, wind up putting two or three trebles into the net behind them. This is a good time to be alone so that no one will laugh at you.

A style that can really produce wild results when fishing near surfaced action involves a jig with a bucktail teaser tied in two feet above the jig. Tie a dropper loop into your main line and add a size 1/0 bucktail or marabu streamer in. If you have some mylar on the streamer, all the better, to create flash attraction.

Now just imagine two five-pound fish, hooked at the same time, with each trying to go exactly the opposite way from each other. Oh my, if you never caught a single one, this double-header could make you talk gibberish for an hour or two because chances are quite good that they will bust you off. Landing a double-header? Possible, sure, and prepare to brag big time if you do.

**#3, Thomas Hill** (660-785-2420) is in the northeast part of the state and it is a reservoir that provides cooling for Associated Electric's coal-fired generators. Hybrids have been stocked here since 1993. Besides live bait, try rattling lures as well as soft plastics.

The list of waters that hold hybrid bass shows Blue Springs Lake as #4, and the state said that fishing prospects from 2004 forward would be very good here. It's in the Kansas City area of the state and for more help, call 816-655-6250.

Try to fish the early spring near the Lake Jacomo spillway at the upper end of the lake after heavy rains. They pop up near the surface in schools at such times. The dam and main lake points are also good in summer and early fall. The "blow hole" is quite good after moderate rainfalls in early mornings. This spot is actually the Jacomo discharge pipe.

**Location #6, Harmony Mission Lake** is also in the Kansas City area and it got a nice stocking of 2,600 hybrid fingerlings in 2003.

Although it's not on the state stocking list, **Norfolk Lake** (in the Ozark Region at the border with Arkansas) sure has lots of white, striped and hybrid bass in it. The upper end of the lake is best in mid-April when sufficient water comes in from Bryant Creek and the North Fork of the White River. The state offers a telephone number for help, 417-256-7161. Just be sure that you are in compliance with all the regulations that apply since you may be in another state's waters!

'04 records show that the state record hybrid bass came out of **Lake of the Ozarks** back on 11/22/86 when Richard Slaybaugh of Kansas City caught his 20½-pound monster.

Besides the web site shown, I got plenty of help from Marlyn Miller, Fisheries Program Supervisor, and Randy Noyes, information specialist with the state. Mr. Miller told me that his state stocked a yearly minimum number of 83,525 to a maximum of 374,470 hybrid bass into their waters over the five year period from 1998 to 2002! Another fine source was the Yearly Fishing Prospects booklet put out by the state. Get a copy!

## MONTANA — NO

Another state that doesn't stock hybrid bass is the fine state of Montana. It's yet another one that sits so far north that chances are pretty good that hybrid bass would not do too well in most of her waters. But that doesn't mean that you should give up trying if you are a resident of this state.

Several years back, the state told me that none would be allowed, under state laws/regulations, without first completing an extensive scientific review. The next step would be to obtain authorization for such a stocking from the Fish, Wildlife and Parks Commission. So, why don't you check out how to do this, and kick it into gear.

It only takes one dedicated person to make a difference, especially if you have friends who are writers and, maybe, know an elected official or two, and perhaps a couple of sporting goods dealers.

## ☑ NEBRASKA — YES

My first shout-out for help in 2002 was answered by Dean Rosenthal, Assistant Division Administrator for the Fisheries Division of the Nebraska Game and Parks Commission. He told me that his state had been stocking 300,000 to 400,000 hybrid bass each year. And these were not fry but instead, bigger babies in the class of fingerling or advanced fingerlings, youngsters with a good survival rate. He listed the lakes that were stocked with hybrid bass in fine detail.

And then as I did the research for this book, Daryl Bauer got my letter and, being a fellow hybrid-hunter, he jumped at the chance to brag about the fine work his state does, and how he catches the fish himself. Daryl is the Lakes and Reservoirs Program Manager so he could even tell folks that he is "working" when out fishing. In fact, he is, hah, "studying," right?

Daryl suggested that folks seeking hybrid bass in Nebraska would be well served by hiring guide Steve Lytle at http://www.stevelytle.com/ According to Mr. Bauer, Steve pursued and actually took the state record at 20.1 pounds back on 8/1/99 out

*Craig Condello caught this 31" striped bass hybrid off Branched Oak Reservoir near Lincoln, Nebraska.*

of Red Willow Reservoir, Steve's favorite hybrid hunting grounds. Daryl told me that Steve or his clients have captured the state record hybrid seven times.

A big Harlan County Reservoir beast broke his standing record one time, but Steve won it back. Red Willow is one of the best places for hybrid in the southwest part of the state and he caught that particular fish on a live shiner, fished deep in the lake.

There are a total of 27 bodies of water in the state that contain goodly numbers of Daryl's "wipers." Most are reservoirs but they also stock heavily-fished recreational sandpits to help area residents enjoy these super fish. Most of the lakes have gizzard shad as main forage, but some contain alewife herring.

A lower number of hybrid bass went in between 2002 and 2004 than had been stocked before, but some of the fish were as long as 7-8 inches. The numbers went from 71,674 to 141,023 in those three years, still plenty.

They began to stock the fish into Bluestem Reservoir, near

Lincoln, in 1979. The state keeps good records of how the fish are doing in each body of water and adds more or less newcomers as needed.

Angler Bauer (as opposed to Program Manager Bauer) likes to catch his hybrid via the use of a pair of waders. He uses a 6½ foot graphite rod with good backbone and a fine spinning reel with large line capacity. Those of you who haven't experienced these critters need to know that lots of line is needed for two reasons: 1) to make long casts, and 2) to handle much longer (as Daryl calls them) "burning runs from big wipers." (Oh yeah!)

He uses 8-pound test line, apologizing for using "heavy" line but he should see the rope that is often used in places like Texas. At times, he uses a heavier rod with Spider Wire Stealth to handle big wipers better. But I don't suggest this for beginners, because that line can cut a slice in your careless fingers with extreme ease as a Rocket takes off.

Some of the tips that Daryl shared with me include the use of a variety of lures. He favors KastMaster and Hopkins spoons as well as Rocket Shad spinnerbaits and a variety of jigs and plugs. Most important to him (and me) is the quality of your hook itself.

Those very nice and skinny Aberdeen types are wonderful for sissy fish like crappie, pickerel, walleye, but a 5-pound hybrid could turn one into a straight pin. So, heavy steel is the answer, a ⅛ ounce saltwater variety of jig is his preference. Funny, I use the exact same jig when fishing for mutton and yellowtail snapper down Florida way, but I add two size 3/0 tag hooks in at the back and bait the threesome with a sardine strip.

Check out the white-cap photo in the Kansas section of Bruce Condello fishing the exact same way as Daryl does. Daryl likes to throw into a lake with wind blowing straight into his face. His favorite reservoir is McConaughy and he will also catch them there on calm days. Jigs are best in the spring, but when the fish are on top, that's the time to chuck out a Pop-R or Chug Bug and try to pop it back to shore. He said that one time, they were so thick that he had a fish on and it got off and before the Pop-R could float to the surface, another Rocket grabbed it.

Boat anglers troll stick baits, but by late summer or early fall, feeding gulls signal where the action is. Deep water trolling works when the fish are down but netting live shad and alewives really is often the top way to go. Make sure you are doing this legally though, check out your rule book, please.

The best time to do this is from July through November and your depth recorder will tell you how deep to fish the live bait. Just don't take too many baitfish, please, and save any that are left over to cut up and use for chum next time out.

Dead frozen bait will work too when the fish are hungry and you may want to try an alternate method. If you are in an experimental mood, thaw out a half-dozen and pick out one that floats to the top of your bucket. Hook it in behind the solid waste dump spot and drop it to the bottom. British folks call this "Pop-up" fishing, and it works wonders. The popping up and down dead bait looks like a dying fish instead. This only works well though when you have double-anchored your boat.

Here's some other waters that offer fine hybrid action in Nebraska, and remember, these are good spots, not mere places that hold some hybrid bass.

There's Branched Oak, Conestoga, and Stagecoach in the Salt Valley Lakes near Lincoln. South-central and south-western area waters include his favorite, McConaughy. Now add a ton of others like Elwood, Johnson, Medicine Creek, Swanson, Jeffrey, Harlan County, (Harlan is really great) Midway, Phillips Canyon, and Lake Helen.

Throw in the Tri-County Canal that runs from Sutherland Reservoir to Johnson Lake. Now add Lake Minatare in the Panhandle. Willow Creek is the only hybrid water in the northeast and Calamus Reservoir is good in the north-central part of the state.

The bottom line is that Nebraska is truly committed to its hybrid bass stocking program, and that sure is good news.

## ☑ NEVADA — YES

Six bodies of water hold state-stocked hybrid bass in Nevada, and in 2004, a new state record was established by Dan Hannum of Dayton in one of them, the Lahontan Reservoir. The 18 and ½-pounder was 33.5 inches long, a "football" indeed.

Mark Warren, Fisheries Staff specialist with the state, as well as his co-worker, Terry Crawford sent me lots of material for the book in 2004. Mark also helped me in 2002 when his title was Sport Fish Staff Biologist.

Back then, he said that they realized what great fish hybrid bass were and reported that the then-record was taken out of the Lahontan that year at 15 pounds. But he sure enough correctly predicted that the record would change, as it certainly did only two years later. In fact, the fellow who got the record in '04 replaced the record that he established the year before at 17.13 pounds.

Besides the Lahontan Reservoir at Churchill County/Lahontan Valley, Nevada stocks hybrid into Washoe Lake (Washoe County), Rye Patch Reservoir (Pershing County), South Fork Reservoir, and

*Dan Hannum holding his Nevada state-record 18½ lb. Rocket.*

Wildhorse Reservoir. South Fork and Wildhorse were just added to the program in 2002 with four-inch fish that have reached impressive size already. And then both lakes got still more large fingerlings in 2003. Best yet, in '04, 10-inch, what I call "Pocket Rockets," went into South Fork and Wildhorse, 1,630 critters in each lake.

The others go back to 1993 when they were first stocked. Washoe has limited forage so the fish don't grow as quickly there but they still reach a nice size soon enough. There are also hybrid bass in the Humboldt River, above and below Rye Patch Reservoir.

Originally, the state got their day-old fish free and only had to pay delivery charges but now they buy them. As done elsewhere, the state gets financial help at times with their program from some Sportsmen's Clubs.

Mark Warren pointed out that Washoe, Rye Patch and Wildhorse each had drought problems for much of the 21st Century so these places were kind of low.

Mr. Warren also told me that the record holder, Dan Hannum, often uses a surface plug in shallow water to catch his wipers, spending many hours to accomplish his chosen goal, catching big fish. Dan had the record for two years in a row and was runner up the year prior. Other successful anglers at Lahontan use large live minnows such as 6-inch carp.

Make sure this is legal at your venue of choice because introducing carp, my second favorite fish, could be illegal in some waters. Largemouth bass anglers feel that carp mess up their bass beds and therefore don't want carp brought into any place that does not have a mess of carp already.

Drifting live bait near bottom off of points of land is a favored style for bait fishermen. Yet another hybrid hunter goes with live minnows held below a bobber where the Carson River enters Lahontan Reservoir. And at all of the lakes, most anglers troll flashers or plugs as well as live bait for optimum success.

I heard from the record holder, Dan Hannum who is, if possible, even more hooked on hybrid bass fishing then I am. Of course, Bill Baab of Georgia and Bruce Condello of Nebraska/Kansas may argue that they are even worse. Dan was referred to me directly by both Terry Crawford and Mark Warren of the state. He agrees that, pound for pound, the hybrid is the hardest fighting fish he too has ever caught, and he has fished all over the west coast and in Mexico. His venue of choice by far is Lahontan.

Dan told me that he had the record fish three years in a row, '02, '03 and '04. In fact his '04 18½ pound hybrid may very well have been bested by another beast he had to the boat that year. But don't you know it, the fish, after a 40 minute struggle, got the plug's hook stuck in the net and the fish shook itself free. Dan felt that it was a 20 plus pounder.

Lahontan is 17 miles long with an upper and lower lake that are connected by narrows. The lake is kind of shallow but reaches 65 feet in a few spots. Targeting hybrid alone, Hannum is still "bothered" often by large walleye.

You can tell the difference in them with ease since a three pound hybrid can drag a six pound walleye behind them at full speed without looking back. I remember catching two 'eyes from 4-5 pounds in the fall of '04 as well as two modest two pound hybrids. Each hybrid stayed on my line longer than both walleye's did all combined.

Dan's large hybrid bass have all come within only two feet of shore and in very shallow water off rocky points that have deep water access. His best months are July and September. Water temperatures in the mid-60's are best and as elsewhere, top times are early morning or late evening.

It is a desert lake and the water warms up a bit too much mid-day. In fact, he has never caught one during mid-day. (Hey, Dan, have you tried to do it during "Solunar Time?" That works sometimes for me.)

Since the lake has no shade, he feels that the fish move into deeper water during the day. And that's when I double-anchor and chum in the deep, looking for the thermocline the fish are holding in, and then I drop my baits to that level, open the drags, and wait 'em out. No, not often, but one hit at high noon can make you very glad you were out there.

Mr. Hannum is so hooked on fishing for these wonderful critters that he sold his home in Lake Tahoe and moved to a small ranch near the lake to run his carpet cleaning business. And when he knocks off for the day, more often than not, he is off to do battle with yet some more Rockets. He estimates that between May and October he fishes 3-5 times a week for them.

No, you don't have to be as whacky about hybrid bass fishing as Dan and I am, but I betcha' that if you hook just one 20-incher, and manage to avoid breaking your line or rod, you may realize why we are so in love with them. "Try it, you'll like it."

## NEW HAMPSHIRE — NO

Sitting way up near the northeast tip of America, here's a state that also is kind of cold to support a hybrid bass fishery. The long and very short of it is that when I asked about the state having hybrid bass in, they told me, plain and simple, twice, no. So the answer is no.

## NEW JERSEY — YES
### *(or should I say Joisey to youze guys?)*

My adopted home state has a wealth of opportunities to present to its anglers. For sure, it has an excellent trout stocking program. And it puts walleye into a few lakes, and a whole gang of lakes get channel catfish. But it also features spectacular saltwater fishing chances to residents and visitors alike.

Containing so many miles of open shoreline from way up in Raritan Bay all the way down to Cape May, it's no wonder that the brine is the area of choice to hundreds of thousands of anglers. But when I am in New Jersey (I run away and hide in Florida for the winter), 99% of my fishing is done in sweetwater. And 90% of that fishing time is spent seeking out hybrid bass, my main fish of choice since I caught my first one back in the early 90's.

New Jersey also stocks northern pike and the muskie/pike hybrid, tiger muskellunge, but the hybrid that I want is the one created out of the crossing of true striped bass and white bass, our own hybrid bass, my Rocket!

*John Korn Jr.'s dad learned him early! Here's Jr. holding a beauty of a Rocket. You just have to trust me when I tell you that there was a rainbow in the background, honest.*

There are three "Pay-Lakes" in the Garden State that contain hybrid bass from time to time. They are Bauer's in Ocean View (609-624-1304), Go Fish in Newton (973-579-6633), and Molders in Jamesburg (732-446-2850). You never know though if a pay lake will get sold to a developer who will build a load of condos around the ponds so call before trying any of these places, please. I remember that Joe Bauer told me that what would have been the N. J. State Record hybrid bass was caught AND RELEASED at one of his ponds in South Jersey back in the late 90's.

The mastermind of the hybrid bass stocking program in New Jersey is dedicated Fish & Wildlife employee, Bob Papson, who from time to time will actually aid in the stocking himself. Bob gave me most of the information that will follow that didn't actually come out of my own head.

The current state stocking list includes three lakes. My favorite is Spruce Run, a 1,290 acre water near Clinton, which is part of

Spruce Run Reservoir State Park.

The biggest lake in the state is Hopatcong at 2,685 or more acres, up in the Morris/Sussex County section of the state. It was initially stocked with hybrid bass by a club that I belong to, the fabled Knee Deep Club, and now the state stocks it with baby hybrids.

Last but not least is the Manasquan Reservoir which is "down the shore," near the Garden State Parkway. This lake closes at dark which makes hybrid hunters leave in an unhappy mood at times but, hey, you can still catch some before dark anyway. This reservoir is smaller at 770 acres.

Some private lakes in the state contain hybrid bass too. Culver's Lake in Sussex County is a closed, private community and only residents are allowed to fish in it. A builder-friend of mine told me that he was involved in the original decision to add hybrid bass into the lake as an attempt at reducing the large numbers of bait fish it contained. No doubt he and his friends had little idea that the state record, a 16 plus beast, would be hauled from their lake.

There have been a few other attempts at stocking hybrid bass into some other waters by the state, but for one reason or another, they struck out. Cranberry Lake, along Route 206 in Sussex County as well as Union Lake in South Jersey at Cumberland County got a load of them, but they are no longer stocked there. And Lake Assunpink also got a bunch, but from what I understand, they are no longer present.

It is my opinion that it's tough to keep hybrid in a lake that has a major outlet towards moving water. And Assunpink drops into Assunpink Creek and then the creek plops into the Delaware River which ultimately joins the Atlantic Ocean in Cape May. Ditto Union Lake. It spills over into The Maurice River which also joins the Delaware and then hooks into the ocean.

So it is possible that all the Assunpink and Union fish eventually ran towards salt, since they are half-striped bass anyway. In fact, New Jersey recently established a new record for salt-water caught hybrid bass. Captain James Fowler was casting a fly from a saltwater pier in Cape May County and bested a 13 pound, two ounce hybrid bass!

Spruce Run was first stocked in 1990 and it gets 12,900 4-inchers yearly. Hopatcong first received state fish in '93 and now gets 26,850 small fish each year. And Manasquan's program began in 1994 and if you do the arithmetic, you will see that all three get 10 fish per acre, as it gets 7,700 yearly.

Fingerlings are obtained by the state from a hatchery in South Carolina and are grown to four-inch size at the Charles O. Hayford Hatchery before being released. I have seen the container trucks at the boat ramp at Spruce Run several times and it still is a great sight to see.

Two guys get into a boat that has a huge container of its own. They load the boat container themselves and ride around the perimeter of the lake, Johnny Appleseed style. They dip large fine mesh nets into the tank and plop 'em overboard. By covering the whole lake with liberal scatterings of small fish, the survival rate is far higher than when too many smaller fish are put into too small an area. This often creates a feeding frenzy in other states involving both fish and birds, and there's nothing good that can be said about baby hybrid bass being gobbled way before their time.

Elsewhere, you will see some of the material that Bill Baab, famous writer with the Augusta Chronicle gave me about the origin of these fish. A study that Bob Papson sent to me, written by R. David Bishop of the Tennessee Game and Fish Commission and presented at the Southeastern Association of Game and Fish Commissioners in New Orleans in 1968 was quite interesting.

Mr. Bishop wrote, in part, that "In early 1965, through correspondence with R. E. Stevens of the South Carolina Wildlife Resources Department, it was decided to hybridize striped bass with white bass. Further, the development of the technique of ovulating striped bass with hormones (Stevens, 1964) produced viable eggs while male white bass were still ripe. Since it made hybridizing an easy process, the experiments were initiated in 1965." And to Mr. Stevens, Mr. Bishop, and their friends, from hybrid lovers like me, Bill Baab, Dan Hannum, Bruce Condello, Ron Bern and countless thousands of others, here's a GIANT "Attaboy!"

You will read elsewhere that hybrid bass are warmwater fish that don't do particularly well in cold water. In fact, I once wrote a column that offered a free autographed copy of one of my books to the first angler who caught a hybrid bass through the ice in New Jersey and could prove it. Well, no one cashed in on that offer that year because most hybrid bass rest in a dormant state in the winter, as do other warm-bodied fish. Yes, some hybrids have been caught through the ice since I wrote that column, but my offer expired, sorry!

Spruce Run Reservoir has a boat rental facility and Lake Hopatcong has two of them, so you don't have to bring your own boat to catch fish at either venue. And to get up-to-the-minute information, try Steve at Lebanon Bait and Tackle, 908-236-9466, (near Spruce Run) or Laurie at Dow's Boat Rentals, on Hopatcong, 1-973-663-3826.

I guess I've taken somewhere in the very lovely neighborhood of 1,750 to 2,000 hybrid bass in New Jersey, but every time, repeat, EVERY time I hook one, another new adventure begins. They truly are as good as it gets, so if you live in a state that doesn't have them, MOVE, or at least visit one that does. Using a variation of what is said in Oregon though, you don't have to make it a permanent move.

## 🚫 NEW MEXICO — NO

This one is a bit tricky. Check your map and you will see that this state sits right where most neighboring states have excellent populations of hybrid bass. In fact, back in the early 90's, I fished several lakes in New Mexico and caught a variety of fish, rainbow and lake trout, as well as salmon.

And when I bought my license, I saw that the name that I thought that I had created, whiper, was already present in the state's compendium of rules and regulations. So I thought that they stocked these fish, as you probably would have too.

But in 2002, they told me that this was because the state's southeast corner butts up to Texas at Red Bluff Reservoir and Texas had hybrids in that lake. Because New Mexico residents had access to these fish, a regulation had to be put into place.

For sure, New Mexico has a very successful true-strain striped bass program in place at its largest reservoir, Elephant Butte Lake. But that doesn't mean that Rockets won't be appreciated if put into one or two selected lakes on a trial basis. Try it, please?

## 🚫 NEW YORK — NO (a/k/a YAWK)

Having been born and raised in the Empire State, I have fond memories of the superb fishing I found in both fresh and saltwater

*Bryan Colley didn't care that New York didn't stock Lake Waccabuc in Westchester County with hybrids when he caught this 15 lb. 5 oz. state record there in 2004.*

there. Giant salmon on Lake Ontario? Beasts of a wide variety in her tributaries? You bet. Muskellunge, pike, walleye, wild trout? Oh my, yes indeed. And that doesn't even include the tuna, shark, cod, striped bass, and so on action found in the brine.

Credit New York with having at least tried to please anglers with hybrid bass efforts in at least two of its waters. The Swimming River Reservoir, upstate New York somewhere or another, was stocked with a bunch of them but the fish apparently escaped, as they tend to do when they find access to moving water.

And Fort Pond, also known as Lake Montauk, had a lot of small hybrid introduced into it as well. These stayed and anyone who caught them there sure was surprised by the spectacular strength of the fish.

The state gave up the program but to this day, some hybrid bass are caught that have escaped from elsewhere, or maybe were illegally stocked. Doug Stang, Chief of the Bureau of Fisheries for New York sent me the accompanying photo of the gentleman who holds the state record on hybrid.

I also found an internet site that showed the photo of a fine hybrid caught from the Chemung River, not far from Elmira, NY, by Gordon Bennett. Gordon wrote that he felt that the fish escaped from a stocking of them some forty miles away in Pennsylvania. So, New York, what do you say, try 'em again?

## ☑ NORTH CAROLINA — YES

When I first spoke to Fred A. Harris, the then-Chief of the Division of Inland Fisheries in N. C. in 2002, I immediately knew that I had a hybrid lover on the other end of the 'phone. Talking about hybrids, Fred described their bite with nearly the following exact words — "They approach a live bait and back up thirty yards to build up a head of steam before charging and hitting."

Fred was a brother Rocket hunter because I have used similar words for 10 plus years to describe how they bite. When I have given seminars about these fish at shows in the Northeast, I usually say something like this:

A hybrid hits so hard that it's almost like they get up to a her-

*Mike's Bait and Tackle in Wilkesboro, North Carolina sent me this snapshot of Michael Gordon with an 8 lb. hybrid, caught March 7th, 2004.*

ring and make an X on their side, then back up 100 feet before beginning their launch into the bait.

So the difference is ten feet and an X; otherwise, we feel quite the same about hybrid bass bites.

Mike's Bait and Tackle (1-336-838-2663) is right at W. Kerr Scott Reservoir at Wilkes, a fine lake that covers 1,470 acres and it gets approximately 10,000 1-2-inch youngsters stocked into it annually. Some other lakes that receive annual hybrid stocking are:

| Water | Location | Acres | Number stocked |
| --- | --- | --- | --- |
| Moss Reservoir | Cleveland | 1,804 | 9,000 |
| Oak Hollow Reservoir | Guilford | 800 | 10,000 |
| Lake Townsend | Guilford | 1,500 | 18,000 |
| Lake Thom-A Lex | Davidson | 650 | 16,000 |
| Salem Lake | Forsyth | 360 | 3,000 |

*Note that Thom-A Lex got more than 24 small fish PER ACRE!*

Robert Curry later became the Chief of the Division and he sent me lots more material. He said that the waters noted above are in the upper reaches of their respective river basins and all are used primarily as municipal water supply. So we have clean water and nice fish, is that ever a fine combination or what?

Lots of methods all work at times for hybrid bass in the state, and it is just about a 365 day a year fishery. You may need to dress up warm in the winter, but you do what you gotta' do, right?

Hybrids tend to migrate upstream in the spring and are caught at the upper ends of the impoundments, as well as in the backs of larger tributary creeks. Their little brains say it's time to spawn and even if they are incapable of doing so, many still chug into such creeks.

Later in the year, especially in late fall and winter, the fish are found in open water. Boaters troll with plugs as well as live bait, and also do well while anchored up with cut bait.

Live shad make the best bait for the biggies, but lots of fish are even taken right from the shore. Nighttime casters sling out a rig baited with chicken liver and while we Rocket anglers try to think our critters are purists, honestly, chicken liver also produces. But you may have to deal with a mess of catfish at night so be careful, please.

Cut bait, as noted above, works from a boat as well as from shore. Try to use just dead bait rather than frozen, but if you only have frozen stuff, it may still work out okay.

Blind casting from shore or boat will produce, but nothing beats throwing into the edge of a feeding school of fish. Anything works when they are busting bait, from bucktails, jigs, crank baits to spoons.

Mr. Curry reported that the state record was taken in 1996 at Lake Chatuge by Michael R. Hogsed and it weighed 17 pounds, 7 ounces. He pointed out that the lake is along the North Carolina/Georgia border, and Georgia takes the lead in the lake's fisheries management.

A few other sources of help for you might be the lake office at Salem Lake — 1-336-650-7677, and WRC Master Officer in District 5, Bryan Scruggs, at 1-919-770-1376.

I fished in Lake Jordan, a 13,900 acre lake that can eat up all six of the smaller lakes noted above, and because of this, I guess, I struck out on hybrid bass. (Hey, you have to have excuses for everything, right?) But this lake, completed in 1981 by the Army Corp. of Engineers, is still noted to contain hybrid bass. I did nail a mess of channel catfish that day on medium-sized shiners, but noted some serious guys trolling past me. My guess is that they were after my favorite fish.

North Carolina is justifiably proud of their hybrid bass program, and they often produce double-figure fish, from 10-15 pounds.

## NORTH DAKOTA — NO

Again, it's way up north, and probably too cold for hybrid bass. But in addition, the state has concerns about even considering adding any because they could stray into Canada.

## ☑ OHIO — YES

If you catch your first hybrid bass in Ohio because you read this book, sure, you can thank me, but don't forget to tip your cap to three guys who work for the state who were very cooperative. They were Division of Wildlife Chief, Michael Budzik, his Program Administrator, John Navarro, and later, Ray Petering, Inland Fisheries Program Administrator.

The division stocks both varieties of hybrid striped bass we have talked about. They are the cross of a female striper and a male white, and the "reciprocal cross," of a female white and a male striper.

There were four lakes that received hybrid bass but one of them, little Kiser Lake in Champaign County at 387 acres, was switched over to pure striped bass stockings in 2005 to give the state brood stock close to their London State Fish Hatchery. But it should still hold hybrid bass, plenty of them, for some years to come. This small lake doesn't allow motors, but at 387 acres, on a quiet day, who needs a putt-putt anyway to break the peace and quiet around you?

The lake was added to the stocking program in 1992 and a mas-

*I don't think this woman caught this hybrid in her swimming
pool in Ohio, no, I don't!*

sive stocking of fingerlings went in during the year 2003 (19,500 in
so small a pond, oh, my!) Friend Navarro suggests the use of
chicken liver at bottom. Some hybrids have been caught here that
hit a full 14 pounds.

Charles Mill Lake in Richland County is one of the three
remaining hybrid-stocked lakes at 1,350 acres. Fishermen do well
with chicken liver here also, from shore as well as from their boats.
The lake has an excellent population of 12 to 22-inchers. The sug-
gestion is to try trolling in summer. Jigging or using night crawlers
also works near shore in spring and fall, especially in the deeper
water near the Marina.

And next comes Buckeye Lake, the largest at 2,847 acres, and
folks with big engines don't have to worry because the lake allows
unlimited horsepower. The lake got its initial stocking of reciprocal
crosses in 2000 when 189,000 went in. Before that the female

striper/male white was used, and since, a mixture of both totaling 240,000 fingerlings were put in the lake.

Yearly stockings vary based on available fingerlings. For example, a whopping 329,000 reciprocal crosses went in. They reach 15-inches in their second year and some are actually taken through the ice here. At such times, go with chicken liver.

Last but not least is East Fork Lake in Clermont County at 2,160 acres. 9.3 MILLION fry were stocked here in a ten year period. And in 2003, another 100,000 fingerlings were put in. Obviously, the overwhelming majority of the fry didn't survive, but, again, 9.3 MILLION, huh?

The overall aggregate number of hybrid bass stocked will be seen a little later on.

3-5-inch live shad that are taken by anglers throwing weighted cast nets produce the top results. And if you can get them, live soft shell crawfish fished at 10-20 foot depths work quite well. When fish are spotted on top chasing shad, anglers catch plenty by heaving jigs or surface stick baits.

When fry are stocked, it is usually in May but the larger fingerlings are added each June.

Mr. Navarro asked me to point out that he encourages his anglers who deep-hook a hybrid on bait to cut their line before releasing the fish. And he didn't say this, so blame me instead of him. It's my opinion that an angler who digs out a ten cent hook from deep within the fish is quite a fool, especially if he releases the fish and then stares in wonder as it pops up in a death swim.

Use unsnelled hooks and have a mess of them at hand so that you can help put a fish back alive to stay. And do handle it carefully, without lifting it up by the line alone, as the weight of the fish could cause irreparable damage to its gut.

The good news is that the state plans to expand its program into yet more inland reservoirs once they further perfect their culture technique for rearing hybrids. Besides rearing some at the London, Ohio Hatchery, many are purchased from the Keo Hatchery in Arkansas.

The division is also proud of their stocking program into a bunch of pools of the Ohio River. They include — Belleville, Gallipolis, Greenup, Hannibal, Meldahl, New Cumberland, Pike Island, Racine, and Willow Island pools. The majority of those that were stocked in the river's pools were reciprocal crosses. Do note that a bunch of these fish make it to Kentucky, just to the south so folks there too should say thanks to Ohio.

And, for sure, if you live near the southeast border with Pennsylvania, you can catch lots of hybrid bass in the Ohio River, courtesy of the stockings of thousands of young hybrid bass that Pa. does in the river. In particular, if you are near Beaver County in Pa., you should have fine access to the fish that Pa. stocks in that area.

Here are the aggregate numbers of small hybrid bass that went into five different bodies of water, courtesy of Mr. Petering — and they sure are impressive. But first, their size-

A "fry" measures an average of ¼ of an inch. A "fingerling" is an-inch and one-half. Some states stock larger fingerlings but Ohio feels that this size works best for them.

| Venue | During which Years | Overall Number |
|-------|--------------------|----------------|
| Kiser Lake | 1992-2004 | 149,889 fingerlings |
| Buckeye Lake | 1989-2004 | 2,312,912 fingerlings |
| Charles Mill Lake | 1997-2004 | 549,829 fingerlings |
| East Fork Lake | 1983-2004 | 289,900 fingerlings plus 20,465,000 fry |
| Ohio River | 1993-2004 | 4,876,407 fingerlings |

Records are made to be broken, of course, but as of the end of '04, Rosemary Shaver held the Ohio record with a 17.68 pound fish that measured a very round 31-inches.

OKLAHOMA

*Cut bait was what guide Clarence Boatman used to beat this 14 lb. beauty in 1998.*

## ☑ OKLAHOMA — YES

Steve Spade manager of the Byron, Oklahoma State Fish Hatchery was quick to provide assistance both in 2002 and again, late in '04 as I began to work on the book. He told me that in one year alone, 2002, his guys stocked the massive total of 896,029 small hybrid bass into 15 reservoirs and lakes. And, no, I don't know who did the actual counting, but if anyone interrupted the guy, a very seriously hurting could have resulted. (joke!)

They started stocking what are called striped bass hybrids in Oklahoma in the mid-70's, and in a ten year period from '92 to '02, better than eighteen million were put in. The state record was set at 23 lbs. 4 oz. a while back and it could have even been bettered by now.

Sixteen lakes in all were stocked with hybrids in 2004 and here's the list Steve gave to me, in alphabetical order:

OKLAHOMA

| Area of state | Name of Lake | Acres | # Stocked | Average Size |
|---|---|---|---|---|
| Southwest | Altus Lugert | 6,260 | 70,900 | 1½-inches |
| Northwest | Birch | 1,137 | 12,000 | 1½-inches |
| Northwest | Boomer | 260 | 5,400 (*) | 1½-inches |
| Northwest | Canton | 7,280 | 80,650 | 1¼-inches |
| Northwest | Carl Blackwell | 3,500 | 34,800 | 1½-inches |
| Northwest | Foss | 8,800 | 44,518 | 1½-inches |
| Southwest | Ft. Cobb | 4,070 | 41,250 | 1½-inches |
| Northwest | G S Plains | 8,893 | 3,000 | 2-inches |
| Northwest | Kaw | 17,040 | 34,238 | 2-inches |
| Central | Konawa | 1,350 | 14,400 | 1½-inches |
| Central | Overholser | 1,500 | 259,140 (**) | 1¼-inches |
| Northwest | Lake Ponca | 805 | 16,100 (*) | 1½-inches |
| Northwest | Skiatook | 10,500 | 108,000 | 1½-inches |
| Northwest | Sooner | 5,400 | 27,200 | 1½-inches |
| Southwest | Tom Steed | 6,400 | 64,500 | 1½-inches |
| South Central | Waurika | 10,100 | 106,320 | 2-inches |

There are some states that mix in fry with fingerling stockings but I think that Oklahoma has a better chance at survival by putting fingerlings alone in, up to two-inches long.

(*) Note the large numbers, twenty per acre, that are stocked into these two small lakes.

(**) And, yes, this number is correct — I talked to Steve Spade who told me that he reared and gave 600,000 small fish to Oklahoma City who stocked close to half of them in this one lake alone. He guessed though that many escaped and went elsewhere, as hybrid tend to do when they can find an outlet. However, just imagine what the fishery will be like there from 2007 on when the remaining ones really grow up!

State regulations were changed at Skiatook in 2002 and because changes are so often made in many states, you should have noticed by now that I have hesitated to show size and bag limits. The last thing I want you to do is get stuck with a fish or two too large, small, or many, and blame "Gone Fishin' ... For Hybrid Bass" for it.

As an example though, at Skiatook, white bass catches were made to be unlimited in total, BUT hybrid catches were limited to a total of five keepers per day and only two of them could reach or exceed 20-inches. And that limit may have been extended to 25-inch fish a few years later so to repeat from elsewhere, know your state's rules always.

I found quite a bit of information about hybrid bass fishing in the www.oklahomagameandfish.com/ok web site (OG&F). In the 12/04 issue, the writer said that Skiatook is one of the best lakes, holding a lot of heavily timbered sections That is, of course, good news and bad.

For bucketmouth bass catchers, it's good, period, but for hybrid hunters, regardless of tackle, heavy stick-ups mean giggling hooked hybrid bass. And they laugh with glee as they tear line off your reel and wrap you around the tree, merry-go-round style, and then break you off.

Clarence Boatman (918-245-3696) guides folks for hybrid bass on Skiatook and he said that shad readings in open water produce far better places to seek out your hybrids in. His clients fish live shad at 20 foot depths, using somewhat heavy line and 3-5-inch baitfish to avoid being pestered by the large numbers of white bass in the lake.

Some sections of the lake that he suggests fishing at are near the Armadillo Island area, Turkey Creek, and the part that goes from Dad's Creek to the dam.

Another place that was brought to my attention in the edition of Oklahoma Game and Fish that I saw is Sooner Lake, in the northern part of the state, 20 miles northeast of Perry. The Oklahoma Gas & Electric Company operates the lake, and some state records have been set at this relatively average sized lake. The northeast corner of the lake is where to go when the power company has their generators pumping water. Fish points of land and visible or submerged islands for yet more action.

David Mitchell is another Oklahoma guide who fishes Sooner

Lake often. Try him at 1-405-720-0907. He too likes larger shad as bait, favoring 4-5-inch baitfish.

Jigging shad-colored slabs and spoons are favored by some anglers in deeper areas of the lake. The only problem with jigging is that if they don't hit quickly, you can get so very, very bored so very, very quickly. OG&F added that fishermen who operate from shore near the warmwater discharge at the northwest part of the lake do well, but they warn that it can be a very long walk before you reach the hot spot. Park at Highway 177 where legal and hike in, bringing someone very strong to help carry everything in and out for you.

In addition to Sooner and Skiatook Lakes, the site showed that Waurika Lake, the last one in our above list, is a particularly fine place to fish for hybrid bass. A guide named Frankie Phelps was quoted as saying that he prefers artificial lures at Waurika because "shad fishing is too easy," and because he fears that many hybrid are killed when taking live bait too deep.

Waurika is 20 miles south of Duncan and was opened in the late 70's to be the water supply lake for that city. Mr. Phelps said that the lake has both gizzard and threadfin shad to help the fish grow big, quickly. His top fish there is a 16-pound slab!

# ☑ OREGON — YES

So, your state is too far north to put in hybrid bass, huh? Well, you cannot get much further north than they do in Oregon, and the state still has a successful program, albeit in only one lake, Anna Reservoir, in the southeastern portion of that lovely state.

Oregon experimented with stockings of hybrid bass at another lake, Thompson Valley Reservoir in 1996 and 1998 but regardless of continued attempts at seeking these fish, the state couldn't find that any were present. So they stopped putting them in and stayed with the success that they found present at Anna Reservoir.

Other stockings of hybrid bass took place at North Tenmile Lake in 1982 and, other than in 1986, continued yearly until 1988. Unfortunately, as is the case in so many venues, these critters tend to stray, especially in spring when they make spawning attempts and go out into adjoining streams and rivers. So you see, they must have all (or at least most) escaped, and that's why they stopped stocking.

Some beast-sized hybrid were still being caught as recently as 2000 when an 18 pound hybrid was nailed. But no one is certain if any more still exist. So let's concentrate on the success of Anna Reservoir now.

Rhine Messmer was the Acting Conservation Biology Section Manager in Portland when I first outreached to the state in 2002, and sure enough, he was still with them in Salem, Oregon provide help two years later in the position of Recreational Fisheries Program Manager. And I also heard from Roger Smith, Klamath Watershed District Fish Biologist.

While Oregon has very cold water, Anna offers fish a better chance at tolerating winter because it is a spring fed system and therefore has water temperatures that allow the fish to survive and thrive. The lake is also is stocked with rainbow trout.

You can plainly tell the difference between a three pound hybrid and a three pound rainbow. The rainbows jump like the dickens, and the hybrids hardly ever do. And the hybrids stay on your line for, maybe, two or three times longer than the 'bows do. I sure do like catching rainbow trout, but, sorry, Trout Unlimited, hybrids fight way, way better, pound for pound.

Anna is only 60 acres in size and is found just north of Summer Lake. It produced the state record hybrid in 2002 at 18.52 pounds for angler Justin C. Marks. Still larger ones have been found during state samplings.

Oregon buys their young hybrid bass from two hatcheries, at times, from one in Arkansas, but usually, from a supplier in Southern California. (Are you listening, California, they are grown in your state for sale, but you don't have any available in your waters for your residents — how come?)

The state had been stocking 2,000 small fish every other year but jumped that up to an average of 9,000 every two years. That's a lot of fish for a small lake, so residents and visitors sure have countless hours of pleasure in store for them.

OREGON · PENNSYLVANIA

The little fish are stocked at an average of 2½-inches in length each, bigger than many states, and they cost approximately a buck per baby to the state.

Mr. Smith told me that there are folks who fish the lake from Lapine, Christmas Valley and Lakeview with good results. Peak effort takes place after waterfowl season ends and late January through early March are some favorite times. This is different from elsewhere when warmer times are generally better. Strange indeed, considering the colder climate.

Fishermen are allowed on Anna Reservoir 24 hours a day and often do best from afternoon into evening. A wide variety of bait produces, ranging from worms, chicken liver, and sand shrimp, to cocktail shrimp. My guess is that a live golden shiner held suspended just off bottom on a slider float will produce some of the biggies. Another popular style here is the use of large plugs while trolling. Casting stickbaits from shore also does the trick.

Anna Reservoir has a very nice boat ramp, with paved access, and for those in need, a nearby toilet facility.

# ☑ PENNSYLVANIA — YES

Here's another of those more northern region states that stocks hybrid bass, and they sure do stock loads of them into quite a few lakes, rivers and reservoirs in Pa. The state also has a successful true-strain striped bass program, proving that both can be stocked in a state with good results.

The Press Secretary for the Pa. Fish and Boat Commission, Dan Tredinnick, was his usual very helpful self when I sought material about his state. When I wrote "Gone Fishin' ... The 50 Best Waters in Pennsylvania," Dan was there with me, step-by-step, providing lots of assistance. He even referred me to the eight area state experts for help with all corners of the state.

And this time, besides the material he provided, he also hooked me up with fellow writer AND GUIDE, Jeff Knapp. Call Jeff at 1-724-465-5555 if you would like to book a trip with him. He likes to fish at both Lake Arthur in Butler County and Shenango Lake in Mercer County.

*Guide Jeff Knapp sent in this shot of a fine hybrid taken in Pennsylvania.*

The lakes/reservoirs that get goodly numbers of 1½ to 2-inch hybrid bass stocked are:

| Lake/Reservoirs | County | Acres |
| --- | --- | --- |
| Lake Arthur | Butler | 3,223 |
| Shenango Res. | Mercer | 3,558 |
| Hammond Lake | Tioga | 640 |
| Lake Redman (Redaman) | York | 290 |
| Blue Marsh Res. | Berks | 1,149 |
| Nockamixon | Bucks | 1,449 |
| Kaercher Creek Dam | Berks | 32 |
| Pinchot Lake (Conewago) | York | 340 |

Lake Erie is the biggest lake in Pennsylvania (no hybrid bass stockings). The state formerly stocked its second biggest lake,

PENNSYLVANIA

Lake Wallenpaupack (5,696 acres), with lots of hybrid bass but now concentrates on putting true strain fish in instead.

There are quite a few moving bodies of water that they stock hybrid bass into, like:

| Water | County | From | To | Acres |
|---|---|---|---|---|
| Beaver River | Beaver | Confluence of Connoquenessing Creek | Mouth of Ohio River | 503 |
| Monongahela R. | Washington | Lock & Dam 4 at Charleroi | Lock & Dam 3 Elizabeth | 1,559 |
| " | Allegheny | Lock & Dam 2 at Braddock | The Point at Pittsburgh | 1,134 |
| Allegheny R. | " | Lock & Dam 2 Sharpsburg | The Point at Pittsburgh | 732 |
| Ohio R. | " | The Point at Pittsburgh | Lock & Dam at Emsworth | 1,027 |
| " | " | Emsworth Lock & Dam at Emsworth | Dashields Lock & Dam at Edgesworth | 1,253 |
| " | Beaver | Dashields Lock And Dam at Edgesworth | Montgomery Lock and Dam at Ohioville | 2,620 |
| " | " | Montgomery Lock & Dam at Ohioview | Pa/Oh Line Line at Glasgow | 1,059 |

So, lake, reservoir or river, you have a wide variety of chances at catching hybrid bass. If I had my 'druthers though, I think that I would opt for a shot at river Rockets. Fighting current sure must make them stronger yet than their lake cousins. I know that river carp fight longer and harder than lake carp do, for the very same reason.

Pennsylvania may very well start rearing their own young hybrid bass at their Huntsdale Fish Culture Station, but they have been able to sustain their program without doing so by trading with other states. Pa. grows their own tiger muskies and other states like Georgia and Tennessee are happy to trade with them. The Keystone State began putting hybrid bass into its waters way back in the 70's.

The state calls these fish "hybrid striped bass" but most local anglers just say "whipers."

Lots of the locations that have hybrid bass in them are listed as being among the top waters in the state for all kinds of fishing in my book, "Gone Fishin' ... The 50 Best Waters in Pa." To get a copy, send $13.95 to me at Box 556, Annandale, N. J. 08801 and I will be glad to mail an autographed copy to you, with no charge for shipping and handling.

Among those sites are Nockamixon, which has four boat access areas. This is one of three lakes that receive true-strain as well as hybrid bass stockings. (The two others are Blue Marsh and Redaman). "Nock" has hybrid bass in it that aren't more than a few pounds under that magic "20" number, because the fish grow to fine size as a result of having access to both alewife herring and gizzard shad to feed on. Horsepower restrictions exist so make sure you are in compliance. Call the state park for current information at 1-215-529-7300.

Blue Marsh goes as deep as 48 feet and is managed by the Army Corp. of Engineers. The fish aren't as big as at Nockamixon, but they sure still please local fishermen. Alewife herring make up the majority of their food. Jeff Knapp suggests using white bucktail jigs, Rapalas, and Sluggos to catch them on artificials. The old standby, chicken liver, works too on bottom.

The lake has two boat launch sites and a modest fee is required but there was no horsepower restriction when we went to print. Check out the lake office for information at 1-610-376-6337.

Pennsylvania doesn't have a listing of hybrid bass in its record keeping, but if they did, the record may very well have been set at Lake Arthur, one of the places that Jeff fishes. Of course you stand a chance at your bait being hit by an overly hungry giant carp. So if your herring gets engulfed and it feels like a very strong and powerful train took off, that may be a "Mr. Man" (carp), not a "Rocket" (hybrid).

Arthur has lots of access sites and has some special regulations on critters like largemouth bass. It holds walleye, true strain muskellunge, channel catfish, and maybe ten other species. It too is in my "50 Best Waters" book. For more on the lake, call the park office at 1-724-368-8811. But don't forget to see if Jeff Knapp has an opening by calling him at 1-724-465-5555.

## 🐾 RHODE ISLAND — NO

I've fished out of Point Judith and caught loads of codfish from that port. Wonderful saltwater action is available to all of the residents and visitors to this little state. But, friends, they just don't put hybrid in, nowhere, no way. The state told me that they don't have any waters that are suitable for such a stocking.

## ☑ SOUTH CAROLINA — YES

SWH is the name that South Carolina's Department of Natural Resources gives to the cross breed in their state. Gene Hayes, Regional Fisheries Biologist for the department was glad to provide assistance regarding their program.

Currently, the state has been concentrating their efforts at stocking loads of fingerlings into two very popular upstate impoundments, Lake Thurmond (Clarks Hill), and Lake Hartwell. In fact, Thurmond received the incredible number of 239,906 1-2-inch fingerlings in 2004, and Hartwell got more yet, 270,073 little guys. In recent years, working together with the Georgia DNR, the goal is to average putting 4 fish in per acre yearly into Thurmond and 5 into Hartwell.

South Carolina began stocking these two waters way back in 1967. The state also stocks true strain striped bass into some waters and also houses a goodly number of natural white perch, as well as white bass.

I spoke to Mike Wilson at the state's facility in Greenwood in the spring of '05 and he provided yet more information about their program. Mike told me that some of the fish that went into Thurmond

*Here's a good example of Lake Hartwell hybrid bass, which can be fished from either South Carolina or Georgia, courtesy of guide Buster Green.*

years back got out below the dam and wound up in the Savannah River.

In fact, the state record came out of the Savannah way back in 1978 when Danny Wood of Commerce, Ga., bested a 20¼ pound SWH. Lake Russell was established some year after the program began and lots of the river trapped fish wound up trapped in Russell. So while Lake Russell has not actually been stocked with hybrid bass, plenty of them are still being caught.

Yet one more lake was shown to contain hybrid bass in an internet sight I found, www.thelunker.net, but Mike was not certain that the state had any involvement with putting them into the lake, called Wylie.

So forgetting Russell and Wylie, let's concentrate our efforts with Hartwell and Thurmond/Clarks Hill, since such huge numbers of fish are available. Both lakes have received either fry or fingerlings on nearly an annual basis for just about forty years now. The fingerlings average an-inch to two inches and are stocked in May.

Thurmond and Hartwell each hold pure striped bass as well as hybrids. For sure, the true stripers can and often do grow far larger. To make note of the difference between the two with extreme ease, look at the stripes themselves.

True strain stripes run from one end to the other in straight lines. And hybrid lines are randomly broken. And if you catch one of each in rapid succession, each weighing, maybe five pounds, it will be easier yet to tell which was which. The hybrid was out there battling you to the boat for twice as long as its true strain cousin.

That lunker web site that I told you about a few paragraphs back said that Thurmond hybrid bass are caught on a variety of lures like Cleos, Berry spoons, KastMasters and white bucktails. They also suggest large minnows, probably meaning golden shiners. Nothing beats a lively herring though, just be sure you have enough oxygen to help these delicate baitfish alive.

Don't just chuck out the dead ones though. They often produce bites, especially if you are fishing on anchor. Those dead herring that float will look alive if you set them up on a slider float and every now and then, pop the rod tip. The dead bait will flip and flop around looking like live bait in trouble, rather than a corpse.

I also found a source for information about Hartwell, which has these critters up to 20 pounds, www.lake-hartwell.com, So it is possible that even before this book sells out and I have to get my printer to crank out another batch, the lake may beat the standing state record. Both shad and blueback herring are the forage base, which sure do contribute to rapid growth. Once again, your bait could be engulfed by a monster-true strain so if so, have your drag adjusted to release line or else a "cow" could break you off in an instant.

Lake Hartwell guide, Buster Green (1-864-277-2463) is one person to contact for help in connection with both hybrid and true stripers. He fishes in a variety of ways so check him out for a fun trip. Lure or bait, he could put you into some beauties.

Buster caught the lake record hybrid, only three ounces under the state record at 20.1 pounds in 1989. And he can remember everything about the fight to this minute. He was fishing down 80 feet over 130 feet of water at night when the beast took hold. It was on his line doggone near as long as the largest pure striper he ever caught in the lake, a 53.2 pound fish in 1987.

## SOUTH DAKOTA — NO

The name includes the word "South," but the state itself is kind of up north, and may not be warm enough for a hybrid fishery. Dennis Unkenholz, Fisheries Program Administrator for the state told me that the forage base there cannot support another predator.

## TENNESSEE — YES

Cherokee Bass are what they call hybrids in Tennessee, for very good reason. The first body of water in America that got hybrid bass was Cherokee Lake in Tennessee, and that was because Dave Bishop, who worked for the Tennessee Wildlife Resources Agency, put the first such little critters into an enclosed pot hole at Cherokee Lake.

Dave had worked with Robert Stevens of the South Carolina Division, to help produce these critters. Mr. Stevens had no facility to grow his young hybrid bass in so he worked with Mr. Bishop to develop the fishery. Dave directly told me that he took the young fish and put them into a 100-acre separate part of the lake to grow in 1965. But that pothole (he called it "The Frog Pond"), overflowed into the main lake and some of the fish traveled out.

At the upper end, by the steam plant at the John Sevier Dam, there is a section of the lake that produces wonderful hybrid bass fishing to this day.

So when you think of whom to thank for your hybrid bass, wherever you live, for sure, thank the person who is in charge of stocking these fish in your waters. But clearly, do remember with thanks the two men who actually were responsible for the whole deal, Robert Stevens and David Bishop.

*TWRA's Eagle Bend Fish Hatchery personnel stocking hybrids into a lake in East Tennessee.*

Tim Churchill was the guy with the state of Tennessee who directed me to Mr. Bishop and also gave me lots of further assistance. He reported that, besides Cherokee, there are three other lakes in his state with aggressive stockings of hybrid ongoing.

The newest addition to the program was Tim Fords Lake at the town of Winchester. This lake was first added to the program in 2002, and by now, some good-sized fish are surely being caught. 25,500 fingerlings are put into Tim Fords yearly.

The three other lakes include, of course, Cherokee (in Jefferson City), which gets 75,500 small fish each year. Further, Boone Lake at Bristol and J. Percy Priest at Nashville get sizeable stockings every year. Boone generally receives 11,300 yearly and Priest, being larger, receives 35,500. Based on availability of stock, there are times that more go into the lakes on an even distribution basis.

The overall numbers of young fish stocked range from 100,000 to 175,000 per year. And these are fingerlings that average approximately three inches each, larger than stocked in nearly all other states, giving them yet a better chance at survival.

In addition to the lakes that have hybrid bass, there are remnant populations of hybrid remaining in parts of the Tennessee and Cumberland river systems, resulting from past stocking efforts. My guess is that these are mostly escapees from one or more of the lakes.

Mr. Churchill told me that the state record was caught at the J. Percy Priest dam on 4/17/98 by Ray Pelfrey and his "Cherokee Bass" weighed in at 23 pounds, three ounces. Tim happened to be there at the TWRA main office when Mr. Pelflrey showed up with his fish and he actually certified the fish himself.

Tennessee hybrid bass are caught in each venue in a variety of ways. For an example, a fisherman named Jay Clementi fishes Priest Lake with a fly rod! I've caught lots of big river carp on a fly rod and I can just imagine how Mr. Clementi has to very carefully manage to avoid getting a "knuckle-buster" injury as the reel revolves backwards with extreme speed.

River salmon anglers who hook fish on fly reels understand it, but still, a Cherokee screaming away on a fly reel, oh, that sounds nice. You sure need lots of extra mono backing to manage to handle the long, blistering runs. Jay is a guide who specializes in putting customers into hybrid bass via the long wand so if you would like to give this a shot, call him at 1-615-429-0172. He also is associated with Orvis, perhaps the best known name in all of fly fishing.

Bank and boat anglers alike catch hybrid bass in the four lakes. Wading is done, especially at sunrise and sunset during spring and fall months. But trolling also produces as does fishing off of lake points of land.

The Tennessee Valley Authority web site rated the hybrid bass (and other) fishing at their lakes in 2003 and here is how they fared. Tim Fords already had a rating of 48 out of a best of 60, even though the program had only recently begun, and Cherokee also was given a 48 out of a possible top of 60.

Cherokee is the largest lake at 30,200 acres in size. Percy Priest is nearly half that size at 14,200 and next comes Boone at 4,520. I didn't get the size of Tim Fords but based on the numbers stocked, my best guesstimate is that it is in the range of 9,000 or so acres.

So wherever you live, give thanks to Tennessee because it all began here in the Frog Pond!

## ☑ TEXAS — YES

Are any of you readers also writers? If so, you may understand this better than most of the other fishermen reading this book. Simply, I shut down for the day after typing these beginning words about Texas, because I just had too much material to go over before delving deeply into preparing this chapter.

You see, Texas stocks an enormous number of her waters with hybrid bass and I have caught them myself in the state so, hey, I'm going to take a break and will see you all at this computer key pad in the morning, okay with you?

Okay, I'm rested up and ready to attack Texas now, with a good night's sleep under my belt so here goes-

In just one year, 2004, the state stocked 27 bodies of water with the incredible number of 4,810,688 little hybrid bass. Just about half of them were fry, with a very modest chance at survival, but 2,303,490 were fingerlings, fish that really had an excellent opportunity to escape predators and other worries. So by now, Texas' waters have yet another gigantic volume of hybrid bass roaming around.

In Bell County, Belton Lake received 99,180 fingerlings, but to enhance the lake's program even further, 1,337,574 fry were added as well. And another lake was given a similar chance. Wichita was stocked with 19,843 fingerlings and another 1,169,624 fry went in.

There are four bodies of water that were each stocked with

TEXAS

*Guide Butch Terpe is holding the hybrid bass that young Corey Buck Covert had just caught on Lake Conroe while trolling Pet spoons behind deep diving crankbaits.*

more than 200,000 fingerlings! They included Cedar Creek Reservoir with the biggest stocking at 326,988, Conroe at 201,554, Lewisville with 295,986, and Richland-Chambers got 205,895.

I have fished Lake Conroe which is up the road from Houston. And, of course, in Texas, "up the road" might mean 75 miles but since the state covers so much land, that's not far.

My separate trips were very different, but in each outing, I caught a bunch of fish, so let me tell you about the varied styles that are put into use at this lake. And no doubt, they would work well elsewhere too because I have caught lots of hybrid bass in other venues using quite similar tactics.

First was with a guy who specialized in hybrid bass, Bob Murphy, who needed to move to the west coast for a while but hopes to return to his favorite honey hole. Bob nets his own bait and prefers to live bait fish on the troll. We used two kinds of bait that he got and each produced results. Shad are probably the main forage fish but we did even better on a variation of golden shiner which are native to its waters. This shiner was different in appearance from the common "roach" and it worked well.

Bob had a supply of bait casting reels that have a built in line counter attached. He could tell just how much line he let go down each time from the contraption that was attached and felt that knowing this gave him quite an advantage.

But more impressive yet was the way that he set up his rod holders in an amazing pattern that let him troll lots of bait. Sure, Great Lakes guys use outriggers and planer boards but I never saw so many lines out in a more normal style than that day. I think we had six baits working at one time.

In season, once the waters warm up, it is common to have three or more fish on at the same time, and that could produce a limit very quickly, but Bob felt that he needed to stick a "school" of bait out to get the fish excited, rather than offering one or two strays. In the start of the book, I talk about this in my part about "Vibration" time. Each rod holder placed baits far enough apart so they could work without tangling and even when a fish hit, we could maneuver around the other rods.

There was a storm brewing so we didn't stay on the water very long at all. But in a short time, I had baits engulfed by five hybrid bass and I managed to boat all of them. Another more modest critter took hold and promptly got off. Bob felt that this was probably a white bass.

We were trolling at pre-determined depths, thanks to the line counter, mid-lake, right near the power lines. My hybrids went up to eight pounds or so, and I stepped onto his dock with a silly grin on my face. And then Bob did this thing that I do not recommend to beginners! He filleted the fish for me to take to my son-in-law's home in Cypress, Texas, with an electric knife, and didn't even lose one finger in the process. Not for me though.

Next time on Conroe was with Bob's friend, Butch Terpe who

actually lives right on the lake. He likes to catch fish, not just hybrid bass, but he sure knows how to put you into hybrids. We fished one spot first for crappie, and nailed a whole mess of slabs, along with some white and yellow bass.

Next came a favorite inshore spot that was covered with fish. Most were hybrid bass, hooray, as well as still more whites and yellows. These first two places were fished with live bait, common golden shiners of modest size. My guess is that, overall, we boated nearly 100 fish! Of course the overwhelming majority were put back.

And then Butch took us to a blue and channel catfish spot and anchored up, putting in a gigantic volume of foul-smelling chum. It didn't take long before the catties bit and he caught a blue cat that topped our fish at maybe 20 plus pounds and released it. We used nasty stink bait absorbed on a piece of sponge. As a variety though, I had a dozen of my own on plain old night crawlers. Call Butch to arrange a trip at 1-936-856-7080.

Lake Conroe offers an enormous amount of open shoreline to fish from, so don't worry about it if you don't have a boat or cannot afford to rent one or hire a guide. Much of the shoreline action comes from channel catfish, but if you can keep a hunk of chicken liver away from them, you might catch a nice hybrid bass on the stuff too. Shore anglers who can cast far out may catch a mess of their own hybrids by using live bait held down via a slider ("slip-bobber") float. This works extremely well, providing you make sure you are off bottom.

So, Lake Conroe for hybrid bass? You bet. But remember, there are 26 other waters that Texas stocks with hybrids so pick one that is close to you and head out for a dynamite day of action. If you would like to get a list of all those waters that are stocked, go to www.tpdw.state.tx.us and poke around. You should be able to find the list if you have any computer skills at all.

And let's refresh a bit regarding what fish is which, because you can get confused, considering the variety that is available in the state.

Yellow bass are easiest to recognize, because they really do have a yellowish tint to their skin. But regarding white and hybrid, besides size (hybrid grow far larger), check out their stripes to truly know one from the other. A white only has one stripe that extends from gill to tail. Hybrids have more than one. Yes, the hybrid stripes may be broken or squiggly, but there still are more than one.

The web site I just referred to offers another means of identifying them, based on a tooth patch that is present on the "tongue" of each member of the clan. True striped bass as well as hybrids have two patches and a white bass only has one.

Another excellent hybrid bass reservoir is Lake Somerville, and having spent a goodly number of years in Somerville, N. J., I liked that name so thought I should tell you more about it. The lake is found about 25 miles southwest of Bryan/College Station, and its 11,460 acres were stocked with 10 fingerlings to an acre in '04, making for a very generous volume of newcomers. The lake is an impoundment of Yegua Creek and offers super fishing for both hybrid and white bass each February, when both fish migrate up that creek.

You can reach the creek from the main lake via boat, but two public areas are also available for folks fishing from shore. The directions are kind of complicated so let me just suggest that you call the Army Corp. of Engineers for them at 1-409-596-1622.

Come summer, the main lake is where the top action can be found. There is plenty of parking, and the charges range from free to five bucks, depending on where you park. And when summer comes, you want to be in the main lake, by boat, or from shore. Shore anglers can set up at Welch Park and fish from shore or do it via wading.

Yet one more wonderful place to catch hybrid bass in is Lake Belton which is situated right dead in the middle of Texas, near Temple, off of Route I35. I talked to Greg at Lock's Taxidermy who told me that guide Jay Garret books trips out of their store (1-254-642-3611). That particular morning, Jay had already left the lake, having pleased his boat load of anglers with a five fish limit for each person.

Jay fishes whichever way his customers wants, more often than not with live shad as bait. He drifts or fishes on anchor and also produces hybrid on cut shad. Belton is 12,000 or so acres and remember that the state not only put a goodly number of fingerlings in during 2004, they also added in excess of one million fry that year!

Here are a few more very good hybrid waters in Texas. Try Ray Hubbard, 30 minutes east of Dallas, and Lake Proctor, near Dublin, Texas. In some years, the state has stocked as many as 41 bodies of water with hybrid bass! Texas Parks and Wildlife Department folks who provided assistance to me were Inland Fisheries Director, Philip P. Durocher and Ken Kurzawski, and to them, a hearty thank you.

# ☑ UTAH — YES

Utah concentrates its hybrid (they call them "wiper") bass stocking efforts at one lake, Willard Bay Reservoir. And as a result of that, they have produced an excellent fishery for her residents and visitors.

When I did the magazine article I talked about earlier, the guy who stepped up to help was Miles Moretti, who was the Assistant Director of the Division of Wildlife Resources for the state. And he was back again with lots more help this time too, wearing the title, "Acting Director." So this material literally comes from "the top." Thanks, Mr. Moretti.

Willard Bay Reservoir is about 20 minutes north of Ogden, Utah and is just off of Route I-15. The lake is 10,000 acres in size at full pool and shaped like a bathtub. The water is somewhat turbid, and the main forage is gizzard shad. The lake also holds walleye, channel catfish, and several other fish.

The Division is very happy with their stocking program, and so too are area residents. The fish haven't grown to particularly large size but, hey, a five pound wiper can sure beat a 10 pound anything else you can catch, just about anywhere. Yeah, maybe a big bonefish can stay with you almost as long as a hybrid, but there just isn't any saltwater near Utah, unless you count that big lake.

*It's kind of chilly in Utah, But the state still manages to stock one
lake, Willard Bay, where Sportsman's Warehouse' Jeremy Adams
caught this fine specimen one evening.*

Chances are quite good that the state record will be broken
before this first edition sells out and I have to go to a second one,
but as we went to print, it stood at 6 pounds 11 ounces and Bret
Felter of Riverdale, Utah holds it with the 26-inch wiper he caught
in 2002. (That broke the record of the top fish Mr. Moretti told me
about when I did the magazine article.) Utah also has records for
the biggest catch and release fish and that was taken by Chad
Chamberlain in 2001, a 23¼-inch Rocket.

The state rears young wipers at its warm water culture facility,
and they also purchase fry elsewhere. 1,000,000 fry have been purchased yearly. Some are stocked right away as fry and lots more

are held to grow to fingerling size.

The stocking program began in 1994 and they put anywhere from 30,000 to as many as 200,000 fingerlings in annually, along with fry, based on rearing success.

The lake sheds itself of ice in either February or March each year and anglers get out as soon as then can, usually starting by trolling. Try trolling the western side of the lake after noon to give you the best chance at slightly warmer water. Pick a sunny day and as you largemouth bass anglers already know, these conditions tend to provide a better shot at fish that are a bit more comfortable. A breeze will help too if it is blowing from the east because that will push warmer water towards the west side.

Trollers pull stuff which imitates the natural forage, gizzard shad. Acting Director Moretti suggests using crankbaits like Rapala Shad Raps or Rat-L-Traps. Go with silver with blue back, or blue with black back and orange belly to imitate the shad. And strangely enough, these anglers go at a pretty fast clip, anywhere from 2½ to 5 mph, producing more strikes than when going slower. Trolling with bucktails will work too, but at slower speeds. Try a ½ ounce marabou jig and add a two-inch Mr. Twister in white onto the hook for added attraction.

The best trolling catches come from mid-May to mid-July, but shore anglers catch them too via casting jigs and crankbaits. Jigs work better from shore, probably because they can be heaved out further.

As found clear across the country, August and September often means boiling fish, with wipers chasing shad up to the top, creating countless surface blasts that can get your heart racing in the blink of an eye. Jigs as well as surface lures work at such times.

Zara Spooks in Pooch and Pup sizes produce, as do Tiny Torpedo's. Little poppers are often engulfed by marauding wipers, and they usually don't suck them down like a sissy trout but rather blast them very hard.

For further help, try calling the Sportsman's Warehouse in Riverdale at 1-801-334-4000.

# ⊘ VERMONT — NO

SMALLMOUTH bass, not hybrid bass, was what John Hall of the Vermont Fish & Wildlife Department wanted to talk about, and justifiably so. Vermont may just be too cold for hybrid bass. But he did tell me that some of the best smallmouth bass action in America can be found in Lake Champlain, in Vermont.

# ✓ VIRGINIA — YES

There are two lakes in Virginia that are liberally stocked with hybrid bass each year. Both are reservoirs that can be found in the southwestern portion of the state. Claytor Lake is on the Ohio River drainage and the John W. Flannagan Reservoir is on the Big Sandy River drainage. The state wants to keep its hybrid bass from heading down into the Chesapeake so they don't put them in further to the east.

Two experts gave me super assistance, the fellows who manage the hybrid fishery at each lake. Thomas M. Hampton is the Fisheries Biologist who takes care of Flannagan and John Copeland is the guy at Claytor.

Flannagan first received hybrid bass in 1999. So, you states who still don't stock them, check out Virginia, they didn't begin to stock this lake until quite recently, and already, lots of fishermen specifically target hybrid bass here.

Only four years after the lake got its first young hybrid bass, a survey showed that 7% of its anglers were already seeking them out on purpose. Fish up to 24 inches were caught in just five years. This lake is found in Dickerson County.

The state buys young hybrid bass at a few different private hatcheries, and stocks Flannagan with 17,000 2½-inch fingerlings each year. These young fish, as also with the Claytor fingerlings, are "Reciprocal crosses," a mix of male striped bass and female white bass, rather than the other and more typical mixture.

Tom really is happy with the instant popularity of the hybrid fishery at Flannagan, and said that he is glad to see folks fishing for them from both shore as well as from a $25,000 boat.

Mr. Hampton said that local anglers quickly get addicted to the

*Here we have two happy anglers catching a Flannagan Reservoir hybrid. By the way, the boy happens to be Tom Hampton's (the fisheries biologist) son Charlie and the man is Tom's father, Charles.*

powerful strike and ensuing battle that only a hybrid catcher can attest to. His fishermen catch them on anything from chicken liver to high-tech plugs. Late evenings are when both live alewife herring as well as chicken liver work.

Anchoring a boat, fore and aft as I always do with *"Gone Fishin',"* and setting floating lights in the water is an exciting method used. You just have to watch out that the Rocket doesn't play swim around the light though because if they are near the top and make a dive around your light cable, you will not only break off the fish but also may get your light wire torn from the battery. So if you hook a hybrid under a light, remove the light from the water to avoid this problem, and keep your stern light on.

If you don't know what I am talking about, check with your

tackle dealer and you will be able to find a gimmick that looks like a truck headlight that is mounted inside of a circular piece of Styrofoam. The light is wired with about a dozen feet of cable and two clips, positive and negative, get attached to your boat battery. Stick the float, light down, in the water, and listen for the sound of drag screaming. And don't worry, I am so very poor with technical things that if I can do it, anyone can.

Claytor is stocked with 33,500 (7.5 per acre) 2-3-inch hybrids each August. It occupies about 21 miles of the main stem of the New River, with one major tributary near the midlake area. Some hybrid bass make the 160 mile journey down the New River and dump into the headwaters of Bluestone Lake in West Virginia. (Check out Bluestone in the West Virginia section.)

Research done at Virginia Tech showed that by putting their young pure striped bass into the lake each June, both babies get a chance at growing without having to compete too much for the same forage. That forage consists of young gizzard shad and alewife herring. But when the whipers grow bigger, they will eat anything they can catch like sunfish and even crayfish.

In the summer, a study by grad student John Kilpatrick showed that hybrid were found in largest number in the water depths of 15-45 feet down while pure stripers needed deeper depths for comfort. The lower third of the lake, between the dam and Claytor Lake State Park, is a good place to fish each summer.

Shallow running plugs produce at night during May and June when the herring are in the shallows to spawn. And early or late each late summer day is when fishermen wait patiently for hybrid to chase either shad or herring to the top. Throwing surface plugs and heavy spoons into the edges of the feeding frenzy will also produce significant slams.

Several students from Virginia Tech have actually published their master's theses about the Claytor Lake fishery! Hybrids up to a dozen pounds have been nailed at the lake. It began to receive fingerlings in 1994 and as noted earlier, John Copeland is the man who gave me material about this lake. One of his sons has been hooked by the hybrid fishery at Claytor. He got the fever with his dad when they were fishing from a state park platform with chicken liver as bait and caught several.

Claytor is stocked with both true striped bass as well as hybrids. It is found in Pulaski County, near the town of Radford. Mr. Copeland actually meets the stocking truck each year and helps distribute the small fish at several boat ramps located around the lake.

## WASHINGTON — NO

Too little forage and too cold water prohibits the addition of hybrid bass into this state. And while there were other reasons given, I won't bother you with them for now.

## WEST VIRGINIA — YES

West Virginia began its hybrid bass program with the initial stocking of youngsters into Bluestone Lake just about thirty years ago, in 1976. The state had been obtaining fry from South Carolina for rearing in special ponds at their Palestine Hatchery in Wirt County. But that may have changed by now because they were soon to complete the new Apple Grove Hatchery in Mason County, where extra pond space would be available.

The state puts a lot of fingerlings into Bluestone but some also get there after a very long swim from Claytor Lake up in Virginia. Bluestone covers over 2,000 acres and stretches over 10 miles in total. Both the New River and Bluestone arms produce hybrid bass. Ramps are present at Bluestone Bridge, Bluestone State Park, Bluestone Marina, Leatherwood Landing, Bull Falls, and at Bertha.

Bret Preston was the Assistant Chief of the Wildlife Resources Section in 2002 when he helped me with my magazine article. And, sure enough, he was back with more assistance three years later.

Besides Bluestone, other lakes that get fingerlings are Beech Fork, East Lynn, Mt. Storm, and R. D. Bailey. Substantial numbers of small fish also go into the tailwater sections of the Ohio and the Kanawha Rivers. A total of 210,000 to 300,000 fingerlings are put into all the waters yearly, based on availability. Yet one more,

*Scott Morrison of WVDNR sent in this great hybrid shot.*

smaller lake received an experimental stocking recently, Dunkard Fork Lake, only 49 acres in size.

The Ohio River gets most of the hybrid bass that are stocked in West Virginia and are joined by lots of young fish that are put in by the state of Ohio, and, for that matter, with sufficient wanderlust, I guess that some Pennsylvania stockies travel to W. Va. as well.

An even dozen places were stocked with small hybrid bass in May and June of 2004. According to an article I read in www.wvgameandfish.com, if you want hybrid bass in the state, a top area would be the tailwaters of the Ohio River dams.

Both Ohio and West Virginia residents may use their fishing

license to hit the Ohio, on either side of the river because of an agreement between both states. You just have to comply with your own state's rules, whichever side you land your fish from.

Three wonderful access points on the river are — The tailrace dam at Belleville Dam, which you can reach via Route 68 near the town of Belleville. The Hannibal Dam is another fine spot on the river and it also offers fishing piers. An outflow is present on the West Virginia side of the river which attracts fish. Get there via SR2 from New Martinsville. And lastly, The New Cumberland Dam can be reached by taking SR2 north out of New Cumberland. A 1½ mile ride will bring you right to the tailwater.

A few more points of the Ohio that are productive include the dam systems at Racine and Robert Byrd. Racine has a power plant that provides warmer water at times but it is on the Ohio side of the river, with good access available. Remember, licensed W. Va. residents are allowed to fish there. The Robert Byrd Locks and Dam are near Gallipolis Ferry, the last dam of the river before it goes into Kentucky.

Noted above, the Kanawha River actually held the standing state records, on length and weight. The longest Rocket was 32.1 inches long and Frankie Harris nailed it in 2000. A bit shorter but more round was the 16 ¾ pound cow that Robert Honaker caught five years earlier.

The lower portion of the Kanawha has three excellent lock and dam systems that all produce good hybrid fishing. They are found at Winfield, Marmet and London. Writer-friend, Jeff Knapp, reported that the pool between the Winfield Dam and the mouth of the river itself was excellent. This dock and dam section has a hydroelectric power plant with good access. Those sections at Marmet and London don't offer as good an access as Winfield does though.

Jeff wrote that Fisheries Biologist Mark Scott told him that R. D. Bailey Reservoir in Wyoming County may be the top hybrid lake in the whole state. The lake is rather deep, with lots of slopes and rocks, ranging down to 70 feet in depth. Areas with clay banks seem to work very well, and as elsewhere, fishing off of points of land will produce. Try bucktail jigs and spoons but also realize that still fishing with bait works very well. Chicken liver and soft-shelled crawfish are very productive baits.

In addition to the two rivers, Bluestone and Bailey, there is another good lake named East Lynn which some feel is as good as any. (Beech Fork also had lots of hybrid bass, but white bass may have moved themselves into this lake in huge numbers). So let's discuss East Lynn. Boat launches are present here at the Lakewide Recreation Area, Lick Creek Launch Area, and at the East Fork Camping Area.

Mt. Storm is yet another fine hybrid lake, which is a power plant lake offering warmer water than elsewhere. So if you want cold times action, hit Mt. Storm, by all means. The hybrids feed on threadfin shad. It's not a producer of big Rockets, but, hey, it has them and when in winter times, you do what you gotta' do to have fun, right?

## ☑ WISCONSIN — YES

The last state in the alphabet that stocks hybrid bass is Wisconsin, located way up in the very top of the country where it can get very cold. So even though it touches Canada and has problems that other states have used as reasons for not putting hybrid bass in, Wisconsin has found one place that can accommodate these super fish, pleasing local anglers all at the very same time.

And that lake is called Columbia, a 500-acre cooling reservoir associated with the Columbia Electric Generating Station near the town of Portage. This is in the south-central part of the state. Karl Scheidegger of the Wisconsin Bureau of Fisheries Management and Habitat Protection was the person who helped me this time. In 2002, it was Steven W. Hewett, Fisheries Policy and Operations Section Chief who was there to provide information.

Mr. Scheidegger said that because of the elevated temperatures in the lake brought about by the cooling process, the lake's waters are sufficiently warm to support a hybrid fishery, and it is the only body that has conditions that will satisfy the needs of hybrid bass in his state.

**WISCONSIN**

Wisconsin began their stocking program in 1981 and numbers stocked vary considerably, based on availability of young fish as well as, at times, a reduction in the lake's forage base. As a result, they have not stocked the lake a few times, and numbers put in, when done, range from as few as 1,000 up to as many as 14,000 yearly.

However, in so small a lake, that is a large number of fish indeed. The babies go from an-inch to as big as five inches long. A hatchery in Virginia provided the initial young fish and the state buys them now from a variety of private hatcheries. Stocking takes place in late June or early July and survival depends on water temperatures when stocked as well as predator densities.

These small fish are fast, but a hungry two-pound anything can still catch a few two-inch fingerlings so they learn quickly to do their wonderful dart and dive thing. Dart & dive thing? Hey, I think that I just made that up, now that I am nearly done with the book, and it was about time. When they grow to line-busting size, hybrid bass can dart this way and dive that way so quickly that you might imagine them being Rocket powered. And that, dear readers, is why I call them Rockets!

Lake Columbia fish are caught in a variety of ways. When the water is warmest and fish are chasing live bait up on top, as they do all around the country, that's the time to sneak up on them quietly. Throw a surface plug and you may not even get to turn the handle twice before it is gobbled down. If you can get some, a live gizzard shad, the natural forage, might not last more than a few seconds when cast into the blitz on top.

The state record has been broken quite often. Three years into the program, a hybrid weighing a little over 11 pounds was taken. Ten years later, in '94, another that was nearly a dozen pounds was caught. And then the numbers kept going up again with four more, still heavier, and as of 2002, the largest weighed 13 pounds, 14.2 ounces. My guess is that you will see one still better soon enough.

Wisconsin has lots of naturally reproducing walleye, muskellunge, and northern pike. But it still made room for my favorite fish in a lake that can accommodate them so that's pretty good!

# WYOMING — NO

Regardless of its wonderful geographic situation, Wyoming has no plans to stock hybrid bass in any of her waters. The comfort that could be available, combined with what would clearly be an extended feeding/growing season, would create some truly outsized hybrid bass here.

But for now, the answer is no. And if you are a resident of Wyoming and would like to do battle with a fish that can, pound for pound, tow a similar sized trout backwards (sorry, 'tis true), write to your Game & Fish Department in Cheyenne and ask them to change their minds.

# Introduction to Afterword

Ron Bern is the guy who is usually seen in the bow of the good ship "Gone Fishin'" when my boat is on a lake in New Jersey. He sets the first of our two anchors (I stick #2 in at the stern), and in general, takes abuse from me all day long. Such is the price a friend has to pay to enjoy hooking up with a Rocket. I rarely, if ever, take anyone else out because they certainly would not tolerate all the orders I throw out this way and that.

My main fishing buddy was a successful business owner who got his Masters in Journalism at the University of South Carolina. He comes from Anderson, South Carolina, and that's why he talks so funny. Ron wrote, ghost-wrote, or co-wrote a whole pile of other books and when I asked him to write this "Afterword," he jumped at the chance, knowing that it would give him a better chance at my being a bit more civil when we fish together. (Not!)

Photo by Manny Luftglass

# Afterword

*By Ronald L. Bern*

*Ron caught this 6 lb. on a slider float at Lake Hopatcong in New Jersey and then he released it, as he does with every one he catches.*

"The surface of the lake is mirror smooth and dusk will soon turn into dark. You're anchored in 50 feet of water and you've already caught and released enough large-mouths and crappie to make a fine day. Then suddenly the gulls go wild, diving repeatedly into a moving spot on the water that is roiling with life. Best of all, they're heading in your direction.

'Fasten your seat belt,' or some such wisdom is uttered by your fishing buddy — in my case, Manny Luftglass — and moments later, your suspended alewife herring go from acting nervous to "making game." The hybrid bass are coming, slashing into a shoal of herring with the gulls picking off the scraps. And judging from the speed and direction of the birds, they're coming fast.

The next sound you hear is the scream of wide-open drags on multiple reels and you're grabbing for the nearest rod to set a hook. If you've got a hybrid on a second rod, or even better, on a second and a third, you are in for the thrill of a lifetime. Your fish tear off in all directions as you try to tighten your drag a little, with one rod in hand and another clamped to your body by an elbow. All the while, you're praying under your breath that you can somehow bring at least one of these beasts under control. The speed of the run and the power of the fish almost defy description. The closest comparison I can make is the rushing power of a big bonefish on the strike. However, after two runs, a bonefish becomes somewhat manageable. A hybrid fights until there is no fight left in him; then he dives under the boat one last time for good measure.

I have caught a 137-pound tarpon on light tackle and more than a few fine bonefish in the Florida Keys; I have caught huge largemouth bass and blue cats in the deep South; I have caught scores of trophy trout and powerful river carp in the fine fisheries of New Jersey and New York. But I can say without qualification that those moments when the seagulls announce the coming of the hybrids, together with the strikes and fights that follow, are unexcelled for pure excitement and pleasure.

I am an angler to the marrow of my bones and there is no species of fish I don't enjoy catching. However, in my book, for pure fishing pleasure, hybrid bass rank first and the best of all the other fresh water fish species are tied for second."


And from your faithful author, that about sums it up as well as anything, right? Now go out and hook a few Rockets, and if you do it all right, you will land the third one after only breaking off the first two!

One last thing, spelling! I won a spelling bee in the fourth grade but in spite of that fine credit, it was just impossible for my computers' spell check to get everything right. So if I messed up the spelling of your favorite lake, lure, a key state employee, etc, forgive me, okay?

*Scuze me, gone fishin'*

# Index

Here are many other great web sites I found:

www.iowadnr.com
www.tri-lakesguide.com
www.wipercentral.net
www.conservation.state.mo.us
www.coloradofisherman.com
www.mississippigameandfish.com

*Florida anglers with striper hybrids at Apalachicola River below Jim Woodruff Dam.*

Photos by Phil Chapman

*Above, happy youngster
with hybrid at Tenoroc
Fish Management Area,
Lakeland, Florida.*

*Photos by Phil Chapman*

# About The Author

**M**anny Luftglass has written thirteen other books, and well over 1,500 columns and feature articles for a wide variety of newspapers and magazines. Former host of a radio show called *"Gone Fishin',"* as well as an environmental and peace activist, he was also a bank director, and President of a newspaper called *"East Coast Angler,"* Manny served the people of Somerville, New Jersey as its elected Mayor through most of the 80's. He has been active with four fishing clubs in the Garden State. A retired Insurance Agency owner, he now likes to say that he is doing now what he likes to do the best — fishing, and writing about it.

# Order Form

For additional copies of this book, any of the twelve other *Gone Fishin'* books, or my book, *So You Want To Write A Book,* please send check or money order to:

**Gone Fishin' Enterprises**
PO Box 556
Annandale, NJ 08801

- New Jersey residents please add 6% state sales tax.
- Tell me who you'd like the book autographed to.
- There will no shipping or handling charges.

For bulk orders call: 908 996-2145

Look up *Gone Fishin'* books at:
**www.gonefishinbooks.com**

-----------------------------------------------------------------

Name: _____

Address: _____

City: _____ State: _____ Zip: _____

Autograph To: _____

*Please send me:*

| # of Copies | Book Title | Price |
|---|---|---|
| _____ | Gone Fishin'... With Kids | $ 9.99 |
| _____ | Gone Fishin'... In Spruce Run Reservoir | $12.95 |
| _____ | Gone Fishin'... For Carp | $12.95 |
| _____ | **Gone Fishin'... For Hybrid Bass** | **$13.95** |
| _____ | Gone Fishin'... Florida's 100 Best Salt Waters | $13.95 |
| _____ | Gone Fishin'... For Beginners | $13.95 |
| _____ | So You Want To Write A Book | $13.95 |
| _____ | Gone Fishin'... In Round Valley Reservoir | $13.95 |
| _____ | Gone Fishin'... In Lake Hopatcong | $13.95 |
| _____ | Gone Fishin'... The 50 Best Waters In Pennsylvania | $13.95 |
| _____ | Gone Fishin'... The 75 Best Waters In Connecticut | $13.95 |
| _____ | Gone Fishin'... In N.J. Saltwater Rivers And Bays | $14.95 |
| _____ | Gone Fishin'... The 100 Best Spots In New Jersey | $16.00 |
| _____ | Gone Fishin'... The 100 Best Spots In New York | $16.00 |